THE COMPLETE KITCHEN

Welcome

Experience tells us the more meals you cook at home, the greater your weight-loss success will be. But what if you've never cooked much before or need help cooking in a healthier way? In this book we'll share all the secrets used in the Weight Watchers kitchen to create our tasty recipes. The first secret I'll reveal is that it's really quite easy. All it takes is a few simple changes to the way you cook and what food you pop in your trolley. The second secret is that our recipes are also delicious and cooking them is part of the pleasure! Enjoy.

LUCY KELLY
Senior Food Editor

ABOUT OUR RECIPES

Flavour comes first

In the Weight Watchers® kitchen we make sure our recipes taste great as well as help you lose weight. For this book we've selected a great range of everyday recipes so you can start your weight-loss journey equipped with easy, tasty meals for any time of day. Each recipe uses basic cooking methods and ingredients that can be found at your local supermarket so mealtimes will be simple and fuss-free.

ProPoints® values

Every recipe in this book has a **ProPoints** value so you can see at a glance how it will work with your personal **ProPoints** budget. This makes meal planning a cinch – just choose your recipes, then cook, eat and enjoy!

▲ Filling & Healthy Foods

We've marked all the **Filling & Healthy Foods** in our recipes with a green triangle ▲. These foods are great for weight loss because they help you feel fuller for longer. As a bonus, they are also lower in sodium, sugar and fat, and/or higher in fibre and/or protein, so they're healthier for you too.

Contents

ONCE YOU HAVE THE RIGHT
INGREDIENTS AND EQUIPMENT, YOU'LL
BE AMAZED AT HOW MUCH EASIER
AND ENJOYABLE COOKING CAN BE!

Getting started

*Whether you've been cooking for decades or just days, learning to cook the Weight Watchers way is easier than you think. While it may require a few changes, the good news is that – just like tracking **ProPoints** values – it's simple once you know how. In this book we share all the tips and tricks you need to know to prepare satisfying, home-cooked meals. In fact, you'll soon forget there was any other way!*

Learning to cook the Weight Watchers way simply involves a few changes to the basic cooking methods used in most recipes. The most important thing is to reduce the amount of fat/oil you use. Grilling, poaching or baking foods are all easy methods of cooking that require little or no additional fat. You can also still pan-fry and stir-fry foods - we'll just show you healthier ways to do it (see p22).

What ingredients you pop in your trolley each week may also require a slightly new approach. Grocery shopping will become an exciting new experience as you shop for our delicious recipes (see p30-153). You'll learn which foods will fill you up without weighing you down and discover tasty low-fat alternatives to your favourite ingredients.

The first step is to organise your kitchen so you have everything you need to get started. Now is a great time to makeover your pantry and fridge (see p10-13) so they are stocked with Weight Watchers friendly foods and the ingredients are easier to find. Also do a stocktake of your cooking equipment, culling anything that is rusty, damaged or just wasting space (olive pitter anyone?). Then check out our must-have kitchen equipment and tools (p14) and identify anything you may need.

There's no need to rush out and buy everything all at once, or cancel all appointments until you get your cupboards in order. Just do things in your own way and at your own pace. But once you have the right ingredients and equipment, you'll be amazed at how much easier and enjoyable cooking can be!

PANTRY MAKEOVER

Spend time organising your pantry and you won't know yourself. First, transfer everything to the kitchen bench. Discard food that is out of date, hasn't been used in the last 6-12 months or has evidence of pantry moths. Vacuum the shelves and wipe them down with hot, soapy water. Re-stack the pantry by grouping similar items together and placing everyday ingredients within easy reach.

Shelf 1

1 Temptation foods: You can still enjoy them sometimes, but those chocolates, lollies and biscuits will be 'out of mind, out of mouth' if you hide them up here. Another trick is to keep 'sometimes foods' in brown paper bags or opaque containers to avoid the visual temptation.

2 Specialty ingredients: Anything you don't use very often, such as cake-decorating supplies, can be archived here. Group like things together in well-labelled boxes or containers. High shelves are also ideal for keeping alcohol out of reach of small children.

3 Food storage supplies: Higher shelves are the best place to keep extra supplies of lightweight items, such as paper towel, foil, plastic wrap, baking paper, storage bags and containers. Avoid storing heavy items up here as you don't want to injure your back lifting them down.

Shelf 2

4 Dry goods: Staples include flour (plain and self-raising), rice, pasta and noodles. Choose wholemeal flour and pasta, brown rice and soba noodles where possible as they are more filling. You might also like to try couscous, polenta and satisfying wholegrains such as quinoa and pearl barley as tasty alternatives to rice. Dried legumes (red, green and puy [French-style green] lentils, black-eye beans, chickpeas, cannellini beans, borlotti beans, yellow split peas etc) are also nourishing fillers that can be added to stews, salads and soups. Store dry goods in clear airtight containers of matching sizes and shapes so it's easy to see when ingredients are running low and they stack neatly on the shelf.

5 Dried herbs & spices: These are great for adding flavour without fat. Handy herbs include thyme, basil, mint, oregano and bay leaves (scatter bay leaves on pantry shelves to keep the moths away). For spices, try cumin, coriander, chilli flakes, cinnamon, cardamom, curry powder, ginger, nutmeg, paprika, Mexican chilli powder, mixed spice, allspice, turmeric, black peppercorns and Moroccan, Tuscan and Cajun seasonings. If kept in airtight containers away from direct heat and light, most herbs will last 1–3 years, while ground spices have a 2-3 year shelf life.

6 Baking ingredients: For basic baking you'll need vanilla essence/extract, bicarbonate of soda, powdered gelatine, cocoa powder, cornflour, sugar (icing, brown, caster and regular), baking powder and desiccated coconut. Store smaller items in baskets or pull-out containers so they are easy to keep organised.

Shelf 3

7 Oils: For low-fat cooking, use cooking oil spray or a teaspoon of canola, sunflower or pure olive oil. A good quality extra-virgin olive oil or linseed oil (also known as flaxseed - keep refrigerated) is best for salad dressings, while sesame oil adds an authentic flavour to Asian cooking. Canola and rice-bran oil are useful when you want a mild flavour or for pan-frying or stir-frying at high temperatures (when other oils may burn).

8 Vinegars & sauces: Vinegars are great as 0 *ProPoints* value salad dressings – balsamic, apple cider, and red and white wine vinegar should cover all bases. A good collection of sauces will also ensure your meals have lots of flavour - try soy sauce, fish sauce, hot chilli sauce, tabasco sauce, Worcestershire sauce, sweet chilli sauce, hoisin sauce and oyster sauce (remember some need to be refrigerated once open).

9 Bottles & jars: Olives, gherkins, capers, sun-dried tomatoes (not in oil), tapenades, salsa, artichoke hearts in brine and baby onions are great for snacks. Bottles of tomato pasta sauce and curry paste are always useful for whipping up a fast meal, while condiments such as pickles, relish and mustard (try wholegrain and Dijon) can add extra flavour to meals without adding too

many *ProPoints* values. Refrigerate after opening.

10 Stock: Tetra packs of chicken, vegetable and beef stock are handy for soups, stews, casseroles and risotto. Choose reduced-salt when you can.

11 Canned food: Cans are terrific for tossing together a quick and easy meal. Where possible, choose reduced-salt varieties for vegies and legumes, and fish canned in springwater or reduced-fat olive oil. Useful cans to keep on hand include: diced tomatoes, tuna, salmon, anchovies, sardines, lentils, butter beans, chickpeas, cannellini beans, black beans, red kidney beans, four-bean mix, baked beans, beetroot, corn, evaporated milk (skim and coconut-flavoured) and light coconut milk. Fruit canned in natural juice (such as apricots, peaches and pears) makes a quick 0 *ProPoints* value dessert.

Shelf 4

12 Breakfast cereals: You're less likely to skip breakfast if something quick and easy is always close at hand. Good choices include traditional rolled oats, bran cereals, wheat biscuits, untoasted muesli and puffed wheat. They'll stay fresher for longer if you decant them into airtight containers.

13 Healthy snacks: When you get the urge to snack, make sure you have healthy choices nearby. Good choices include: plain microwave popcorn, crispbreads, rice cakes, wholegrain crackers, Weight Watchers snack foods, non-creamy instant soups, and small amounts of dried fruit (pitted dates, banana chips, apricots etc), and unsalted nuts and seeds (almonds, Brazil nuts, cashews, walnuts, pistachios, pepitas [pumpkin seed kernels] and sunflower seeds).

14 Everyday items: Life is just easier if you store the things you use every day within easy reach, such as bread (wholegrain or rye is more filling), tea, coffee, low-joule spreads, Vegemite, honey, salt, pepper, and sugar or sweeteners.

Bottom shelf/floor

15 Potatoes & onions: Store potatoes, onions, sweet potato, garlic and uncut pumpkin at the bottom of your pantry. Choose containers where they will stay cool, dark and dry and have plenty of ventilation (lidded baskets are ideal). Onions and potatoes should be stored separately so they stay fresh for longer.

16 Heavy bottles: Large bottles of diet soft drink, mineral water, diet cordials and water are best stored on the floor so they won't fall off and squash your toes!

FRIDGE MAKEOVER

One of the main benefits of organising your fridge is that you can see what you have (or don't have) at a glance. Start by taking everything out and discarding anything past its use-by date. Clean the shelves, walls and drawers with warm, soapy water, then wipe dry with a cloth sprinkled with vanilla extract to give it a fresh aroma. Re-stack the shelves by grouping like items together.

Top shelf

1 Everyday items: This shelf is closest to eye height so it's perfect for storing regularly used items such as Weight Watchers Canola Spread, dips (low-fat hommus and tzatziki), low-fat mayonnaise and sandwich fillings (such as lean sliced ham, bacon, pastrami and smoked salmon).

2 Eggs & tofu: It's not ideal to store eggs on the door as the constant movement and temperature changes can affect the quality. Keep eggs in their carton so they don't absorb odours from other foods. Tofu (firm and silken) is great for meat-free meals. Once opened, place it in an airtight container and cover with water, then use within four days.

3 Dairy products: Cold air vents are usually located near the top of the fridge so store highly perishable items such as dairy products here. Good choices for weight loss include: skim milk, low-fat yoghurt, extra-light sour cream and reduced-fat cheese (tasty, cottage, ricotta and feta). Parmesan cheese is also handy for sprinkling on pasta and salads as it's only used in small amounts.

Middle shelf

4 Leftovers: Store leftover meals and half-used ingredients on this shelf. Keep them in airtight containers and place them at the front so you don't forget they are there. Alternatively, transfer the food to a small ceramic plate and cover with plastic wrap - this often makes the food look more appetising and reminds you to eat it. Leftovers should be eaten within two days, except for rice which should be eaten within 24 hours as it can contain a type of bacteria that can survive reheating. Always reheat leftovers until steaming hot, and do not reheat them more than once.

5 Sometimes food: Use the room at the back of this shelf for things that are used less frequently, such as jars of anchovies or that box of chocolates you'd rather not see. Get into the habit of regularly rotating the contents of your fridge so you know which ingredients are nearing their use-by date.

Bottom shelf & crisper

6 Fresh meat & seafood: Cold air from the top vents falls, so the bottom shelf is the best place for lean raw meat, poultry, fish and seafood. It also means raw juices can't drip onto other foods and cause cross contamination. If you are not cooking it that day, transfer meat or seafood from its packaging or bag and place on a ceramic plate before covering with plastic wrap. When thawing raw food, sit it on a tray to catch any drips.

7 Crisper drawers: If you have two crisper drawers, use one for vegetables and herbs and one for fruit. This is because some fruits produce a gas (ethylene) that can cause vegetables to deteriorate faster. Vegies that are prone to drying out or wilting will keep longer in the crisper if stored in sealed plastic bags with most of the air expelled (for herbs, remove the rubber bands and wrap in paper towel first). Handy herbs include fresh flat-leaf parsley, mint, coriander, oregano and rosemary. Fresh ginger is useful, too. However, choose your fruit and vegetables according to what's in season so it tastes better, lasts longer and is at its nutritional peak (see p18).

The door

8 With all that opening and closing, the fridge door experiences the most temperature variation so contrary to popular belief it's not ideal for storing highly perishable products such as eggs, milk and dairy. Instead, use the door pockets to store cold drinks and opened bottles and jars (chutneys, relish, mustard, pesto, tapenade, tomato paste, curry pastes, capers, anchovies and gherkins etc), oil-free salad dressings and Asian sauces (such as hoisin, oyster, teriyaki and sweet chilli).

The freezer

9 There is no real science to organising a freezer. Just remember square-shaped containers take up less room than round or uneven shapes and always label everything (with the date and number of serves) so you know what's what and when it should be used by. It is also important to freeze food as soon as possible (allow freshly cooked food to cool first). Wrap it well and expel as much air as you can to prevent freezer burn (when ice particles form on the surface, which affects the texture and taste). See p160 and the table below for basic guides to freezing food.

Some useful items to keep in your freezer include:

Bread: Sliced wholegrain, Turkish, pita, tortillas, sourdough or wholegrain rolls, wholemeal crumpets and multigrain English muffins.

Fat-free fruit sorbet: Any flavour.

Frozen pastry: Reduced-fat shortcrust and puff.

Frozen fruit: Raspberries, blueberries and cherries.

Frozen vegetables: Peas, green beans, corn, cauliflower, broccoli, Brussels sprouts, spinach and stir-fry mixes.

Low-fat ice-cream: At least 97% fat free.

Lean meat: Such as chicken breast fillets, beef mince and steaks, lamb leg steaks and mini roasts, and pork fillets and stir-fry strips.

Fish & seafood: Firm white fish fillets (such as snapper, ling, blue-eye trevalla and flathead) and peeled green prawns.

Homemade chicken and beef stock.

Weight Watchers frozen meals and desserts.

MEAT FREEZING GUIDE

Type	How long?
Raw beef, lamb or pork roasts	4–12 months
Raw beef, lamb or poultry mince	3–4 months
Raw beef, lamb or pork steaks	6–12 months
Raw beef, lamb or pork chops	4–6 months
Raw beef, lamb, pork or chicken strips/ diced meat	2–3 months
Raw pork mince	2 months
Bacon	1 month
Raw sausages	1–3 months
Raw chicken pieces	6–9 months
Raw whole chicken	12 months

ESSENTIAL EQUIPMENT

They say a cook is only as good as their equipment and that's certainly true when cooking the Weight Watchers way. With the right equipment you can cook with less fat and ensure your portion sizes are spot on. Here are our kitchen must-haves.

* Products shown are available exclusively at Weight Watchers meetings.

COOKING SPRAY OIL*
A light spray on the cooking surface is all you need – a clever way to reduce the amount of oil in your cooking.

NON-STICK FRYING PANS AND WOK
Non-stick cookware is best because it requires only a minimal amount of cooking oil, plus it's easier to clean.

MICROWAVE OVEN
For everyday fat-free cooking of rice, porridge and vegies, reheating frozen portions and leftovers, or popping corn without oil.

PAPER MUFFIN/ CUPCAKE CASES
No need to grease muffin or cupcake holes, plus washing up is much easier.

METRIC MEASURING JUG
For easy, accurate measurement and dispensing of liquid ingredients.

BAKING PAPER
For lining cake tins, baking trays, baking dishes and even barbecue plates so you need less oil and have an easier clean up.

MEASURING CUPS*
An accurate way to measure dry ingredients such as flour and sugar.

ELECTRONIC KITCHEN SCALES*
Indispensable for precise weighing every time.

Other essentials include:

- 3 chopping boards (always use different boards to prepare raw meat or fish, vegetables and ready-to-eat food to prevent cross-contamination)
- 3 saucepans with lids (large, medium and small)
- colander
- sieve
- box grater
- microwave-safe dishes
- electric rice cooker

- 2 large baking trays
- 1 stovetop chargrill pan
- 4 stirring spoons (2 wooden, 2 large metal)
- 2 baking dishes
- meat thermometer
- plastic wrap, snap-lock bags, foil and paper towel (for blotting fat)
- food processor or stick blender
- electric beaters
- cake/muffin tins and wire racks
- mixing bowls
- rolling pin and scone cutter.

SILICONE UTENSILS
If you're using non-stick cookware, you'll need these so you don't damage the special surface.

CITRUS MICROPLANE
An easy way to add highly flavoured zest to cakes, biscuits, sauces, puddings, crumb toppings and rice and couscous dishes.

HOLD HERE
This area stays cool during cooking

CAUTION — HOT ST
open carefully away from bod

easy fast simple
Steam Bags

STEAM BAGS*
For fast, fat-free and mess-free cooking in the microwave.

SILICONE BRUSH
For controlled application of oil on grill plates and other cooking surfaces.

BAMBOO AND/OR METAL STEAMER
Both are great as a fat-free cooking method for vegies, fish, poultry and more. Bamboo steamers sit over a wok, while you can buy metal steamer baskets to fit inside your existing saucepans.

MEASURING SPOONS*
We use Australian standard measuring spoons, where 1 tablespoon equals 20ml (UK and US tablespoons are only 15ml).

CITRUS JUICER
For extracting fresh juice for dressings, baking, desserts and marinades.

MANDOLIN OR V-SLICER
Finely shaves vegies and fruit (such as fennel or apple) for salads.

VEGETABLE PEELER
An everyday preparation utensil that's also great for making 'ribbons' from cucumbers and other vegies.

GOOD-QUALITY SHARP KNIVES
A 20cm chef's knife will do everything from trimming and dicing meat to chopping vegies.

MANAGING YOUR KITCHEN

*The best way to keep your fridge and cupboards neat and tidy is to plan your meals. That way you'll only buy what you need and never have to scramble through the shelves searching for something to eat. With a bit of forward planning you'll also save time, money and **ProPoints** values!*

Meal planning

Planning ahead is one of the key tools for weight loss, and that includes writing a weekly menu. Use this and other recipe books to decide what you want to eat, then make a shopping list. This will not only ensure that you have the right ingredients but most people find they spend less when they shop with a list.

When selecting recipes for your menu, try to concentrate on those with lots of **Filling & Healthy Foods** (highlighted with a green triangle ▲ in all our recipes). They will keep you feeling fuller and satisfied for longer, while also helping you make healthy choices that are low in *ProPoints* values. **Filling & Healthy Foods** include fruit, vegetables, low-fat dairy products, lean protein (lean meat, fish, skinless chicken breast, legumes, tofu and eggs) and wholegrain foods (such as rye and high-fibre bread, cereals, wholemeal pasta and brown rice) and are a great way to bulk up your meals.

Also try to cook as seasonally as you can. For one thing you will enjoy more variety, rather than cooking the same meals week-in, week-out. Buying foods in season also means that they are at their flavour peak and will probably be cheaper because supply is plentiful. See p18-19 for a month-by-month guide to what's in season.

Shopping tips

To make your shopping trip quicker and to avoid forgetting things, divide your list into sections such as fruit and vegetables, dairy, bakery, meat and fish, pantry and frozen items. When shopping, always check the use-by dates and buy the items with the longest shelf life. Avoid damaged packets and dented cans as air may have affected the contents.

Shop for non-perishable food first and pick up cold, frozen and hot food last (even if it means going in the opposite direction to everyone else!). Ensure cold food feels cold, frozen food isn't too icy (which suggests it may have defrosted at some stage) and hot food feels sufficiently hot. Be wary of freezer and chiller cabinets that are stacked right to the top - the 'load limit' line should be visible otherwise the cabinets may not have enough power to keep food cold enough. Pack perishable items straight into cooler bags and get home as soon as possible so you can get them into the fridge.

More simple tips

Eggs: Ideally eggs should be sold in refrigerated cabinets to maximise their shelf life. Weight Watchers recipes use eggs with an average weight of 59g (usually sold as 'extra large'). Always open the box and check for cracked shells before buying.

Fruit, vegies & herbs: Buy sturdier vegetables, such as potatoes, carrots and pumpkin first, then pick up more delicate produce (such as lettuce, berries and herbs) so they don't get squashed in your basket. Select unblemished produce and gently touch soft fruit such as peaches, plums and avocados to gauge their ripeness. Some fruits, such as mangoes, pineapples and melons, should also smell as ripe as they look. Choose bunches of herbs that are fresh and glossy.

Fish & seafood: Look for fish fillets with firm, bright flesh and no discolouration. Whole fish should have lustrous skin or scales, bright eyes and pinky-red gills. Select crustaceans (such as prawns and crabs) and molluscs (mussels, squid, octopus, oysters, scallops, cuttlefish or clams) with brightly coloured shells or flesh that is firm and intact. All fish and seafood should have a pleasant but not strong smell of the sea.

Lean meat: Choose meat that is bright in colour, with no hints of discolouration, and avoid packets that are leaking. When selecting lean meat, look for cuts with the least visible white fat on them. These tend to come from the inner parts of the animal as they generally store fat under the skin and this translates to having a strip of fat along the

BUYING SEASONAL FRUIT AND VEGIES IS A GREAT WAY TO ADD VARIETY TO YOUR MEALTIMES AS THE CHOICES ARE CONSTANTLY CHANGING.

edge of a chop, steak or slice of bacon. The cuts that are naturally lean (and the most tender) are the fillet and loin cuts of red meat, and the breast meat of chicken and turkey.

Leg meat from pork, lamb and beef also tends to be quite lean once the exterior fat is trimmed away. But keep an eye out for any fat within red meat (called marbling), which tends to come from the shoulder area or animals that have been bred and fed to achieve this effect. If you can keep these differences in mind, it may help when you next need to come up with an instant substitution at the supermarket.

Portion sizes

Always include the weight of the ingredients you need on your shopping list. Sometimes it might seem cost-effective to buy more because it's on special or only available in bulk, however, don't be tempted to use more than the recipe asks for. When cooking the Weight Watchers way it's important to stick to the correct portion sizes so you don't accidently consume more *ProPoints* values than you are actually tracking.

In our recipes we've worked out all the portion sizes for you but you still need to use measuring spoons, scales and a measuring jug to ensure that you are accurate. One of the most useful tools is a set of Weight Watchers electronic scales (see p14), which not only weighs food but also calculates the exact *ProPoints* values for you.

When you're not following our recipes it's important to get the balance right on your plate. You might be used to filling half your plate with protein and the other half with vegies and carbohydrates (such as pasta or potato). But it's better to cover half the plate with vegies and make one-quarter lean protein and the other quarter starchy carbohydrates (such as rice, pasta, noodles or potato). Choose wholegrain varietes where possible. See diagram below.

VEGETABLES AND SALAD

LEAN PROTEIN

STARCHY CARBOHYDRATES

SEASONAL PRODUCE GUIDE

January

FRUIT
apricots
bananas
blackberries
blueberries
cherries
figs
grapes
limes
mangoes
melons
nectarines
oranges
pawpaw
peaches
pears
pineapple
plums
raspberries
strawberries

VEGETABLES
beetroot
cabbages
capsicums
celery
corn
cucumbers
eggplant
green beans
lettuce
peas
radishes
tomatoes
watercress
zucchini

February

FRUIT
apples
apricots
bananas
blueberries
figs
grapes
limes
mangoes
melons
nectarines
oranges
pawpaw
peaches
pears
pineapple
plums
raspberries
strawberries

VEGETABLES
Asian greens *(such as bok choy and choy sum)*
beetroot
cabbages
capsicums
celery
corn
cucumbers
eggplant
garlic
green beans
leeks
lettuce
peas
pumpkin
radishes
tomatoes
watercress
zucchini

March

FRUIT
apples
bananas
blueberries
custard apples
figs
grapes
limes
melons
nashi
nectarines
oranges
pawpaw
peaches
pears
pineapple
plums
pomegranates
raspberries
strawberries

VEGETABLES
Asian greens *(such as bok choy and choy sum)*
avocados
beetroot
broccoli
capsicums
celery
corn
cucumbers
eggplant
garlic
green beans
leeks
pumpkin
radishes
snow peas
tomatoes
zucchini

April

FRUIT
apples
bananas
custard apples
figs
grapes
kiwifruit
lemons
limes
melons
nashi
passionfruit
pawpaw
pears
pineapple
pomegranates
quinces

VEGETABLES
Asian greens *(such as bok choy and choy sum)*
beetroot
broccoli
Brussels sprouts
cabbages
cauliflower
capsicums
celery
corn
garlic
leeks
peas
parsnip
pumpkin
sweet potatoes *(kumara)*
zucchini

May

FRUIT
apples
bananas
custard apples
grapes
grapefruit
kiwifruit
lemons
limes
mandarins
nashi
oranges
passionfruit
pawpaw
pears
persimmons
pomegranates
rhubarb
rockmelon

VEGETABLES
Asian greens *(such as bok choy and choy sum)*
broccoli
Brussels sprouts
cabbages
cauliflower
celery
fennel
ginger
leeks
parsnip
pumpkin
spinach
sweet potatoes *(kumara)*

June

FRUIT
apples
bananas
custard apples
grapefruit
kiwifruit
lemons
limes
mandarins
melons
nashi
oranges
passionfruit
pawpaw
pears
persimmons
rhubarb
rockmelon
strawberries

VEGETABLES
Asian greens *(such as bok choy and choy sum)*
beetroot
broccoli
Brussels sprouts
cabbages
capsicums
cauliflower
celery
eggplant
fennel
green beans
leeks
parsnips
pumpkin
spinach
sweet potatoes *(kumara)*
zucchini

You can buy carrots, onions and potatoes all year round but many other fruit and vegies taste better – and are often cheaper – if you buy them during their peak growing season.

July

FRUIT
apples
bananas
custard apples
dates
grapefruit
kiwifruit
lemons
limes
mandarins
melons
oranges
passionfruit
pawpaw
pears
rhubarb
strawberries

VEGETABLES
Asian greens *(such as bok choy and choy sum)*
broccoli
Brussels sprouts
capsicums
cauliflower
celery
eggplant
fennel
green beans
leeks
parsnips
pumpkin
spinach
sweet potato *(kumara)*
zucchini

August

FRUIT
apples
bananas
custard apples
dates
grapefruit
kiwifruit
lemons
limes
mandarins
melons
oranges
passionfruit
pawpaw
pears
strawberries
rhubarb

VEGETABLES
Asian greens *(such as bok choy and choy sum)*
beetroot
broccoli
Brussels sprouts
capsicums
cauliflower
celery
eggplant
fennel
green beans
leeks
parsnips
pumpkin
silverbeet
spinach
sweet potato *(kumara)*
zucchini

September

FRUIT
apples
bananas
custard apples
grapefruit
kiwifruit
lemons
oranges
papaya
passionfruit
pawpaw
pears
mandarins
melons
rhubarb
strawberries

VEGETABLES
artichokes
asparagus
beetroot
broad beans
broccoli
Brussels sprouts
capsicums
cauliflower
eggplant
fennel
garlic
green beans
peas
pumpkin
spinach
zucchini

October

FRUIT
bananas
blueberries
grapefruit
kiwifruit
lemons
mandarins
mangoes
melons
papaya
passionfruit
pawpaw
pears
pineapple
rhubarb
strawberries

VEGETABLES
artichokes
asparagus
beetroot
broad beans
broccoli
cabbages
cauliflower
cucumbers
green beans
leeks
peas
pumpkin
watercress
zucchini

November

FRUIT
bananas
blueberries
cherries
grapes
grapefruit
kiwifruit
lemons
mangoes
melons
oranges
papaya
passionfruit
pawpaw
pineapple
raspberries
rhubarb
strawberries

VEGETABLES
artichokes
Asian greens *(such as bok choy and choy sum)*
asparagus
beetroot
broad beans
broccoli
cabbages
cauliflower
corn
cucumbers
green beans
leeks
peas
watercress

December

FRUIT
apricots
bananas
blueberries
cherries
figs
grapes
kiwifruit
mangoes
melons
nectarines
oranges
passionfruit
pawpaw
peaches
pineapple
raspberries
rhubarb
strawberries

VEGETABLES
Asian greens *(such as bok choy and choy sum)*
asparagus
beetroot
broccoli
cabbages
capsicums
cauliflower
celery
corn
cucumbers
green beans
leeks
peas
tomatoes
watercress
zucchini

OUR RECIPES ARE ALL ABOUT EASY COOKING TECHNIQUES AND INGREDIENTS YOU CAN FIND AT THE SUPERMARKET SO ANYONE CAN CREATE A NUTRITIOUS MEAL.

Cooking basics

Now your kitchen is organised and you've planned the week's meals, it's time to get cooking. If you're not used to cooking from scratch this may seem a bit daunting but with our simple techniques and step-by-step recipes you'll soon be whipping up meals with ease. So grab your apron and let's get started!

We know that not everyone is a wanna-be chef. But with Weight Watchers recipes you don't have to be. Our recipes are all about easy cooking techniques and ingredients you can find at your local supermarket so anyone can create a tasty, nutritious meal. Here are some basic tips to get you started:

- Before you begin, read your chosen recipe from start to finish so you know exactly what ingredients and equipment you'll need and what order you need to do things in.
- Get your ingredients and cooking equipment out before you start cooking. This will save you time and makes cooking easier because everything is within easy reach.
- If you want to brown something, make sure the pan is hot before you add your ingredients (food should sizzle as soon as it hits the pan).
- Don't overcrowd the pan when browning meat and poultry. If you do it will stew in its own juices rather than browning and may become tough and chewy.
- Try not to turn or move meat too soon when browning it – it needs time to form a good seal. You can tell when meat is ready to turn if it no longer sticks to the pan and releases without effort.
- If you need boiling water at any stage of the recipe, put the kettle on before you start cooking so it is ready when you need it.
- Have a sink full of hot soapy water so you can wash up as you go (and wash your hands easily if needed). That way you won't be left with all the washing up to do after your meal.
- Think about batch-cooking (doubling a recipe so you can chill or freeze half for another meal). It's barely any extra effort, but double the reward!

STEP-BY-STEP COOKING

STIR-FRYING

Stir-frying can be done in a large non-stick frying pan or a wok.

1 *Cut ingredients into small, similar-sized strips or pieces so they cook evenly. Make sure all your ingredients are ready before you start cooking, because once you begin there is no time to stop.*

2 *When you are ready to stir-fry, heat your frying pan or wok over high heat. Add 1–2 teaspoons oil and swirl to coat. Alternatively, lightly spray the ingredients with oil.*

3 *Cook ingredients in small batches, moving them constantly from the centre of the pan to the sides so they don't burn. If food starts to stick, add a tablespoon of water rather than more oil. Keep the first batch warm while you cook the rest.*

STEAM-FRYING

Similar to stir-frying but uses less oil and is great for vegies.

1 *Again, cut ingredients into small, similar-sized strips or pieces so they cook evenly. Make sure all your ingredients are ready before you start cooking.*

2 *Lightly spray the frying pan or wok with oil and heat over high heat. Start by stir-frying the ingredients until lightly browned. Start cooking harder vegies such as onions and carrots before softer vegies.*

3 *Add 2–3 tablespoons of water, cover with a lid and cook until the water has evaporated and the ingredients are tender. Add more water if needed.*

GRILLING

Grilling can be done in a chargrill pan, on the barbecue or under a stove grill.

1 *Preheat the pan, barbecue or stove grill to the required heat. If it's not hot enough when you start cooking the meat will stew in its own juices.*

2 *Lightly brush or spray the food with oil and cook on both sides until cooked to your liking. Only turn the food once and resist the urge to poke it as this can make the food tough and chewy.*

3 *After grilling, always 'rest' meat or chicken so the meat fibres relax and the juices are reabsorbed. To do this, transfer the meat to a plate and cover with foil. Set aside for 5 minutes before serving. The meat will then be tender and juicy when cut.*

POACHING

Poaching can be done in a large saucepan or a deep frying pan with a lid.

1 Fill a large saucepan or deep frying pan with 5cm (about 2L) of water or stock.

2 Add some herbs and spices if you wish (eg 1 sliced eschalot, 1 clove, a few black peppercorns, a sprig of fresh thyme and parsley, and a bay leaf), then season with sea salt and bring to the boil. If using herbs and spices, simmer, covered, for 15 minutes to release the flavours.

3 Reduce heat so liquid is barely simmering and add even-sized fillets of chicken breast or fish. Cover and poach until cooked (about 10 minutes for 125g chicken portions and 5 minutes for 150g pieces of fish).

ROASTING

Roasting can be done in an oven or a covered barbecue.

1 Preheat the oven or barbecue before cooking. For an oven this usually takes about 15 minutes, depending on the temperature required. A covered barbecue will take longer.

2 To roast meat or chicken, place it in a baking dish and lightly spray or brush with oil. The dish should only be slightly larger than the food being roasted or the juices will burn on the base of the pan. If cooking vegetables without meat, use flat baking trays lined with baking paper (the low sides will achieve a crispier finish).

3 After roasting, always 'rest' meat or chicken so the meat fibres relax and the juices are reabsorbed. To do this, remove the cooked meat from the baking dish and cover with foil. Set aside for 10–15 minutes before carving. The meat will then be tender and juicy when you slice it.

Which setting for roasting?

The fan forced feature of the oven produces a faster, drier heat and is good for browning and crisping. Convection heat (when the fan is off) is a little slower and more gentle. It is often good to start roasting large joints of meat with convection heat and then use fan-forced heat for the last 15 minutes to brown and caramelise the ingredients.

How do I know if it's cooked?

When roasting meat the best way to tell whether it is cooked is to use a meat thermometer. If you don't have one, you'll need to be guided by recipe cooking times.

Whole pieces of red meat can be eaten still pink in the middle but rolled/minced meats and chicken should be cooked all the way through (to test chicken, pierce the thickest part of the thigh and make sure the juices run clear).

ROASTING GUIDE

1.5kg whole chicken	1¼ hours at 200°C
1.5kg leg of lamb	1½ hours at 200°C
1.5kg beef rump, sirloin, scotch or fillet	1 hour at 200°C

FOOD PREPARATION TIPS

You don't have to slice vegies like a chef to cook a great meal but try these tips to make preparation quick and easy.

Asparagus: Hold each stalk with both hands and bend until it snaps. Discard the woody ends.

Avocado: Cut the avocado in half. Hold the half with the stone in one hand and carefully tap it with a sharp knife so it sticks in the stone. Twist the knife to pull out the stone, then use a spoon to scoop out the flesh in one piece. Cut as required.

Butternut pumpkin: Cut in half and scoop out the seeds with a spoon. Use a swivel-headed peeler to easily remove the tough skin.

Capsicum: Cut in half through the stem, then remove and discard the seeds and white pithy sections.

Chillies: If you like the flavour but not all the heat of chillies, cut them in half lengthways and scrape out the seeds and white pithy membranes (wear gloves or rinse hands well afterwards so you don't rub chilli in your eyes or nose).

Eschalots: The thin papery skin on eschalots (also known as French shallots) is quite tricky to peel off. It's much easier if you put them in a heatproof bowl and cover them with boiling water for 1-2 minutes to loosen the skin first.

Garlic: Some garlic crushers will squeeze unpeeled garlic and leave the papery skin behind. If yours doesn't, trim off the base of the clove and place it on a chopping board. Cover the clove with the flat side of a large kitchen knife and press down with the heel of your hand until the clove 'pops'. This will loosen the skin and make it easy to remove. If you don't have a crusher, sprinkle finely chopped garlic with salt, then press on it with the flat side of a large knife until it forms a paste.

Leeks: Remove the dark green tops and roots (you only want the thick pale section), then cut vertically from the top, almost to the base. Wash under the tap, fanning out the layers to release any trapped dirt. Shake dry before slicing.

Mango: For sliced mango, use a small sharp knife to peel the mango, then slice off each 'cheek' (thickest part of the mango either side of the stone) and cut into slices. For mango chunks, simply cut the unpeeled cheeks from either side of the stone and score a diamond pattern through the flesh (but not through the skin). Use both thumbs to push up the skin side of each mango cheek and slice off the chunks. In both cases, don't forget to cut the rest of the flesh from the stone.

Mushrooms: There's no need to peel or wash cultivated mushrooms, simply trim the stalks and wipe the tops with damp paper towel.

Onions: Slice off the top (pointy end), leaving the root attached. Cut the onion in half, through the root, and discard the papery skin. The root then holds the onion together as you slice or chop it, making it much easier to handle. To finely chop the onion, place it cut-side down on a board and, holding your knife parallel to the board, make one or two horizontal cuts towards the root (don't cut all the way through). Then turn the knife and make thin vertical cuts from the root to the top of the onion. Finally, slice across the onion to release the pieces (see photo, at right). Discard the root.

Pineapple: Trim off the top and base. Stand pineapple upright then cut down the length of it to remove the skin (especially the 'eyes'). Cut pineapple in half, then cut each half into wedges. Cut out the tough core.

How to cook grains, legumes, rice and pasta

UNCOOKED	COOKED	COOKING METHOD	ProPoints
Couscous: 1 cup (188g)	2 cups (310g)	Place couscous in a medium heatproof bowl. Add 1 cup (250ml) boiling water. Stir briefly to combine, then cover and set aside for 3–5 minutes or until liquid has absorbed. Scrape with a fork to separate grains. Reheat in microwave or steamer if required.	Serves: 6 2 *ProPoints* values per serve
Quinoa: 1 cup (185g)	3 cups (450g)	Rinse quinoa in a sieve under cold running water. Drain. Place in saucepan with 2 cups (500ml) lightly salted water. Bring to the boil. Reduce heat and simmer, covered, for 15 minutes or until water has absorbed. Remove from heat and set aside for 5 minutes to allow the residual heat and steam to finish off the cooking.	Serves: 6 2 *ProPoints* values per serve
Pearl barley: 1 cup (200g)	3 cups (570g)	Rinse pearl barley in a sieve under cold running water. Drain. Place in saucepan with 2½ cups (625ml) lightly salted water. Bring to the boil. Reduce heat and simmer, covered, for 30 minutes or until liquid has absorbed. Remove from heat and set aside for 5 minutes to allow the residual heat and steam to finish off the cooking.	Serves: 6 2 *ProPoints* values per serve
Polenta: 1 cup (170g)	3 cups (750g)	Bring 3 cups (750ml) lightly salted water to the boil in a large saucepan over high heat. Gradually add polenta in a thin, steady stream, whisking until polenta is incorporated into water. Reduce heat and simmer, stirring constantly, for 10 minutes or until polenta is thick and soft. Add extra water if necessary during cooking.	Serves: 6 4 *ProPoints* values per serve
White rice: 1 cup (200g)	3 cups (510g)	**ABSORPTION:** Place rice in saucepan with 1½ cups (375ml) lightly salted water and bring to the boil. Reduce heat and simmer, covered, for 12 minutes or until just cooked. Remove from heat and set aside for 10 minutes to allow the residual heat and steam to finish off the cooking. **BOILING:** Place rice in a medium saucepan. Add 2L (8 cups) lightly salted water. Bring to the boil. Reduce heat slightly and gently boil, uncovered, for 12–15 minutes or until tender. Drain. **RICE COOKER:** The easiest way to make perfect rice every time. Follow rice cooker instructions. Rice cookers are available at supermarkets and electrical stores.	Serves: 6 4 *ProPoints* values per serve
Brown rice: 1 cup (200g)	3 cups (510g)	**ABSORPTION:** Place rice in saucepan with 1½ cups (375ml) lightly salted water and bring to the boil. Reduce heat and simmer, covered, for 25–30 minutes or until just cooked. Remove from heat and set aside for 10 minutes to allow residual heat and steam to finish off the cooking. **BOILING:** Place rice in a medium saucepan. Add 2L (8 cups) lightly salted water. Bring to the boil. Reduce heat slightly and gently boil, uncovered, for 25–30 minutes or until tender. Drain. **RICE COOKER:** The easiest way to make perfect rice every time. Follow rice cooker instructions. Rice cookers are available at supermarkets and electrical stores.	Serves: 6 3 *ProPoints* values per serve
Dried legumes (*borlotti, cannellini, lima, red kidney and black-eye beans, chickpeas and brown, green and red lentils*): 1 cup (200g)	Approximately 3 cups (260g–600g) depending on the type of pulse	Place beans in a large bowl and cover with room-temperature water. Set aside to soak overnight (this makes them easier to digest). To cook, discard soaking water and rinse. Place beans in a large saucepan and add enough lightly salted water to cover by 10cm. Bring to the boil. Reduce heat and simmer until tender (see time guides below). Drain. *Chickpeas and borlotti, lima, cannellini and red kidney beans* (soak overnight) – 1 hour. *Black-eye beans* (no soaking required) – 30 minutes. *Red lentils* (no soaking required) – 12–15 minutes. *Green lentils* (no soaking required) – 25 minutes. *Brown lentils* (soak for 2 hours) – 30 minutes.	Serves: 6 2 *ProPoints* values per serve
Dried pasta: 250g	500g	Bring 2L (8 cups) lightly salted water to the boil in a large saucepan. Add pasta and cook following packet instructions or until just tender (see time guides below). Stir the pasta as you put it into the water to stop it clumping together but do not add oil or your sauce won't stick. Drain. *Spaghetti and farfalle* – 12 minutes. *Penne* – 11 minutes. *Spirals, macaroni and tagliatelle* – 10 minutes.	Serves: 4 5 *ProPoints* values per serve
Dried Asian noodles (*egg, hokkien or wheat*): 250g	500g	Bring 2L (8 cups) lightly salted water to the boil in a large saucepan. Add noodles and cook following packet instructions or until just tender. Stir the noodles as you add them to the water to prevent clumping. Drain.	Serves: 4 6 *ProPoints* values per serve

Flavour basics

Salad dressings

ITALIAN DRESSING

 ProPoints VALUE PER SERVE
SERVES: 4

   1 tbs extra-virgin olive oil
   2 tbs balsamic vinegar
▲ 1 garlic clove, crushed

1 Whisk all ingredients in a small bowl.
Drizzle over salad just before serving.

FRENCH DRESSING

 ProPoints VALUE PER SERVE
SERVES: 4

   1 tbs extra-virgin olive oil
▲ 2 tbs lemon juice
   1 tbs white wine vinegar
   2 tsp Dijon mustard
▲ 1 garlic clove, crushed

1 Whisk all ingredients in a small bowl.
Drizzle over salad just before serving.

SWEET CHILLI & LIME DRESSING

 ProPoints VALUE PER SERVE
SERVES: 4

   1 tbs sunflower oil
   1 tbs sweet chilli sauce
▲ 2 tbs lime juice
   2 tsp soy sauce

1 Whisk all ingredients in a small bowl.
Drizzle over salad just before serving.

Sauces

TOMATO PASTA SAUCE

 ProPoints VALUE PER SERVE
SERVES: 4

   2 tsp olive oil
▲ 1 brown onion, chopped
▲ 1 garlic clove, crushed
   1 tbs tomato paste
▲ 400g can diced tomatoes
▲ 1 tsp dried Italian mixed herbs
   2-3 tsp red wine vinegar
   1 tsp sugar

1 Heat oil in saucepan over medium heat.
Cook onion, stirring, for 5 minutes or until
softened. Add garlic and paste and cook for
1 minute. Add tomatoes, herbs, vinegar and
sugar and bring to the boil. Reduce heat
and simmer, covered, for 20 minutes.
NOTE: Use for pasta, fish, chicken or veal
or add to casseroles and soups. Store in an
airtight container in the fridge for up to
3 days, or freeze for up to 3 months.

HEALTHY WHITE SAUCE

 ProPoints VALUES PER SERVE
SERVES: 4

▲ 2 cups (500ml) skim milk
▲ 1 onion, chopped
▲ 10 black peppercorns
▲ 1 fresh or dried bay leaf
   2 tbs cornflour

1 Place 1½ cups (375ml) milk, onion,
peppercorns and bay leaf in a saucepan.
Gently stir over low heat until almost
boiling. Remove from heat. Set aside for
15 minutes. Remove onion, peppercorns
and bay leaf with a slotted spoon.
2 Whisk cornflour and remaining milk in
small bowl. Stir into hot milk mixture. Cook,
stirring, over low heat for 3-4 minutes or
until thick and bubbling. Season with salt
and pepper.
NOTE: Use for macaroni cheese, pasta
bakes and tuna mornay.

Stock

CHICKEN STOCK

 ProPoints VALUES PER CUP
MAKES: 2L (8 CUPS)

   8 chicken wings or 2 chicken
     carcasses (see note)
▲ 3 carrots, chopped
▲ 3 celery sticks, chopped
▲ 1 onion, quartered
▲ 2 fresh or dried bay leaves
▲ 4 sprigs fresh thyme
▲ 12 black peppercorns

1 Place all ingredients in large saucepan.
Add 2.5 litres (10 cups) water. Bring to the
boil. Reduce heat and simmer for 1 hour,
skimming off scum from the surface.
2 Strain stock into a heatproof bowl. Discard
solids. Place stock in the fridge. Once cool,
remove solidified fat from the surface.
NOTE: You can use the carcass from roast
chicken to make stock. Or ask your butcher
or chicken shop for uncooked carcasses.

It's easy to add flavour with minimal fat. Use these basic recipes to add that special something to simple salads, plain pasta and grilled chicken, meat or fish.

Marinades

LEMON & CHILLI MARINADE

 ProPoints VALUE PER SERVE
SERVES: 6

- 1 tbs sunflower oil
▲ 1 tbs lemon juice
▲ 1 tsp finely grated lemon rind
- 1 tsp sambal oelek
▲ 2 garlic cloves, crushed

1 Whisk all ingredients in a medium glass or ceramic dish.
NOTE: Add 750g firm white fish fillets or lean chicken breast fillets and toss to coat. Cover and refrigerate for 20 minutes, then chargrill or barbecue.

HONEY SOY MARINADE

 ProPoints VALUES PER SERVE
SERVES: 8

- ⅓ cup (80ml) soy sauce
- ⅓ cup (80ml) honey
- 1 tbs sesame oil
▲ 2 tsp finely grated fresh ginger

1 Whisk all ingredients in a medium glass or ceramic dish.
NOTE: Add 1kg lean chicken breast fillets or pork fillets and toss to coat. Cover and refrigerate for 20 minutes, then chargrill or barbecue.

GREEK MARINADE

 ProPoints VALUE PER SERVE
SERVES: 4

▲ ⅓ cup (80ml) lemon juice
- 1 tbs extra-virgin olive oil
▲ 1 garlic clove, crushed
▲ 2 tsp dried Greek oregano

1 Whisk all ingredients in a medium glass or ceramic dish.
NOTE: Add 500g diced lean lamb leg or pork fillet and toss to coat. Cover and refrigerate for 20 minutes. Thread onto skewers before cooking on a preheated chargrill or barbecue.

Herb & spice rubs

BARBECUE SPICE RUB

 ProPoints VALUE PER SERVE
SERVES: 4

▲ 1 tbs sweet paprika
- 3 tsp onion powder
- 1 tsp garlic powder
▲ 1 tsp dried thyme leaves
▲ 1 tsp dried oregano leaves
- 1 tbs brown sugar

1 Combine all ingredients in a small bowl. Spoon into an airtight container and store in a cool, dry place until ready to use.
NOTE: Rub over 500g lean beef, lamb, chicken or pork, then chargrill, roast or barbecue.

MOROCCAN SPICE RUB

 ProPoints VALUE PER SERVE
SERVES: 4

▲ 1 tbs cumin seeds
▲ 2 tbs coriander seeds
▲ 12 saffron threads
▲ 2 tbs sweet paprika
▲ 2 tsp dried chilli flakes

1 Heat a small frying pan over medium heat. Add cumin and coriander and cook, stirring, for 1-2 minutes. Transfer to a mortar and pestle and crush until coarsely ground. Add saffron, paprika and chilli and stir to combine. Cool. Spoon into an airtight container and store in a cool, dry place until ready to use.
NOTE: Rub over 500g lean lamb, beef, chicken or prawns, then chargrill, roast or barbecue.

Simple sides

Easy salads

GARDEN SALAD

 ProPoints VALUE PER SERVE
SERVES: 4

- 4 cups (120g) lettuce (such as baby cos, iceberg or oak leaf), torn into bite-size pieces
- 1 Lebanese cucumber, halved, sliced
- 250g cherry tomatoes, halved
- 1 green capsicum, sliced
- 1 cup (40g) alfalfa sprouts
  1 tbs olive oil
  1 tbs balsamic vinegar

1 Combine lettuce, cucumber, tomatoes, capsicum and sprouts in a large bowl. Drizzle with oil and vinegar and toss to combine. Serve.

GREEK SALAD

 ProPoints VALUES PER SERVE
SERVES: 4

- 4 tomatoes, chopped
- 2 Lebanese cucumbers, cut into chunks
- 1 red onion, sliced
  1 tbs olive oil
  1 tbs red wine vinegar
  12 kalamata olives, not in oil
  80g reduced-fat feta cheese, crumbled
- ½ tsp dried oregano

1 Combine tomatoes, cucumber and onion in a large bowl. Drizzle with oil and vinegar. Top with olives and sprinkle with feta and oregano. Serve.

COLESLAW

 ProPoints VALUE PER SERVE
SERVES: 4

- 2 cups (160g) shredded wombok (Chinese cabbage)
- 1 cup (80g) shredded red cabbage
- 1 large carrot, cut into matchsticks
- 3 green shallots, thinly sliced
  ¼ cup (60ml) low-fat mayonnaise
- 2 tbs lemon juice
  1 tbs white vinegar

1 Combine wombok, red cabbage, carrot and shallots in a large bowl. Whisk mayonnaise, juice and vinegar in a small bowl. Add mayonnaise mixture to cabbage mixture and toss to combine. Serve.

Basic vegies

STEAMED GREENS

 ProPoints VALUE PER SERVE
SERVES: 4

- 200g green beans
- 200g sugar snap peas
- 2 cups (240g) frozen peas

1 Fill a saucepan with 7cm water and bring to the boil. Place beans and sugar snap and frozen peas in a steamer basket. Place basket over boiling water and steam, covered, for 5 minutes or until vegies are bright green and just tender.

VEGIE STIR-FRY

 ProPoints VALUE PER SERVE
SERVES: 4

  2 tsp sesame oil
- 2 green shallots, sliced
- 1 red capsicum, sliced
- 150g fresh or thawed frozen broccoli florets
- 150g green beans, cut into 3cm pieces
  2 tbs oyster sauce
  2 tbs soy sauce

1 Heat a wok or large non-stick frying pan over high heat. Add sesame oil and heat for 5 seconds. Stir-fry shallots, capsicum, broccoli and beans for 3 minutes or until tender. Add oyster and soy sauces and stir-fry for 2-3 minutes or until heated through. Serve.

ROASTED VEGETABLES

 ProPoints VALUE PER SERVE
SERVES: 4

- 1 red capsicum, cut into 3cm pieces
- 1 red onion, cut into thin wedges
- 300g button mushrooms
- 500g pumpkin, cut into 3cm pieces
- 1 eggplant, cut into 3cm pieces
- 2 zucchini, thickly sliced
- 250g cherry tomatoes
  1 tbs extra-light olive oil
- 2 garlic cloves, crushed

1 Preheat oven to 200°C or 180°C fan-forced. Line 2 baking trays with baking paper. Combine all ingredients in a bowl. Season with salt and freshly ground black pepper. Arrange on prepared trays. Bake for 35-40 minutes or until tender and golden. Serve.

*We've given some classic side dishes a Weight Watchers makeover so you can still enjoy all your favourites for less **ProPoints** values.*

Potatoes

MASHED POTATO

 ProPoints VALUES PER SERVE
SERVES: 4

▲ **600g potatoes, chopped**
▲ **⅓ cup (80ml) skim milk**

1 Boil, steam or microwave potatoes until tender. Drain. Mash in a large bowl with milk and a pinch of salt until smooth. Serve.

ROAST POTATOES

 ProPoints VALUES PER SERVE
SERVES: 4

▲ **4 x 120g potatoes, cut into 4cm pieces**
  1 tbs extra-light olive oil

1 Preheat oven to 200°C or 180°C fan-forced. Line a baking tray with baking paper. Steam, boil or microwave potatoes until partially cooked. Drain and toss with oil.
2 Place potatoes on prepared tray and bake for 45-55 minutes or until golden and crisp. Serve.

JACKET POTATOES

 ProPoints VALUES PER SERVE
SERVES: 4

▲ **4 x 150g potatoes**

1 Preheat oven to 200°C or 180°C fan-forced. Place potatoes in a large baking dish and lightly spray with oil. Roast for 1 hour or until tender. Cut a deep cross in the top of each potato and gently squeeze base to open. Serve.
NOTE: To save time, pierce potatoes with a fork and microwave on High (100%) for 5 minutes, turning halfway through. Bake for 30 minutes or until tender.

Gravies

CLASSIC GRAVY

 ProPoints VALUE PER SERVE
SERVES: 4

  Cooking juices from roast chicken
    or meat
  1 tbs cornflour
  2 cups (500ml) chicken or beef stock

1 Use a spoon to skim off any fat from cooking juices. Alternatively, pour into a jug and place in the freezer for 10 minutes to allow fat to rise and solidify, then spoon off fat. Return juices to flameproof baking dish. Combine cornflour and stock in a bowl.
2 Heat baking dish over low heat. Gradually stir in stock mixture. Increase heat to medium and cook, stirring constantly, for 1-2 minutes or until gravy boils and thickens. Serve.

ONION GRAVY

 ProPoints VALUE PER SERVE
SERVES: 4

  2 tsp sunflower or canola oil
▲ **1 brown onion, sliced**
  2 tbs gravy powder
  2 cups (500ml) boiling water

1 Heat oil in medium saucepan over medium heat. Cook onion, stirring, for 5 minutes or until softened and golden.
2 Combine gravy powder and water in heatproof jug. Pour into saucepan and cook, stirring, for 1-2 minutes or until thickened. Serve.

WHETHER YOU RISE EARLY OR LATE,
A TASTY AND FILLING BREAKFAST
SHOULD ALWAYS BE YOUR FIRST
APPOINTMENT OF THE DAY.

Quick & easy
BREAKFASTS

Wholemeal breakfast pizza

 ProPoints VALUES PER PIZZA | **MAKES:** 4 | **PREP:** 10 MINS | **COOKING TIME:** 10 MINS

4 x 46g small wholemeal pita breads

⅓ cup (80ml) tomato pasta sauce

▲ **4 slices (60g) Weight Watchers Bacon, fat trimmed, coarsely chopped**

▲ **2 roma tomatoes, thickly sliced**

⅓ cup (40g) Bega So Extra Light grated tasty cheese

▲ **½ cup (15g) baby spinach leaves**

Filling & Healthy Foods are marked with a green triangle. These foods help fill you up and keep you healthy.

1 Preheat oven to 200°C or 180°C fan-forced. Lightly spray a large baking tray with oil. Place pita breads on prepared tray and spread with pasta sauce. Top with bacon and tomatoes and sprinkle with cheese. Bake for 10-12 minutes or until cheese is golden and bases are crisp.

2 Cut each pizza into quarters. Serve topped with spinach leaves.

WHO SAID PIZZA WAS JUST FOR LUNCH OR DINNER? WITH A SIMPLE TOPPING OF BACON, TOMATO AND MELTED CHEESE, YOU CAN ENJOY IT ANY TIME YOU PLEASE!

Toasted muesli

ProPoints VALUES PER SERVE | **SERVES:** 10 | **PREP:** 10 MINS | **COOKING TIME:** 15 MINS

▲ **3 cups (270g) traditional rolled oats**
1 tbs sunflower seeds
⅓ cup (35g) chopped walnuts
2 tbs honey
2 tbs maple syrup
1 tbs pepitas (pumpkin seed kernels)
1 tbs linseeds (see note)

Filling & Healthy Foods are marked with a green triangle.
These foods help fill you up and keep you healthy.

1 Preheat oven to 180°C or 160°C fan-forced. Line
a large baking tray with baking paper. Combine
oats, sunflower seeds, walnuts, honey and maple
syrup in a large bowl.

2 Spread oat mixture in an even layer on prepared
tray. Bake, stirring occasionally, for 15-20 minutes
or until golden and crisp. Stir in pepitas and
linseeds. Allow to cool. Serve.

NOTE: Linseeds (also called flaxseeds) are
small brown seeds with a high oil content and
are best stored in the fridge. Find them in the
health-food section of most supermarkets or
from health-food stores.

SERVE WITH: ½ cup (125ml) skim milk,
2 tablespoons low-fat vanilla yoghurt and 2 small
pieces fresh fruit (chopped), such as banana, pear
or mango. Add 2 **ProPoints** values per serve.

▶ **TIP**
*You can store this muesli in an
airtight container in the fridge
for up to 2 weeks.*

Poached green eggs & ham

 7 ProPoints VALUES PER SERVE | **SERVES:** 2 | **PREP:** 10 MINS | **COOKING TIME:** 10 MINS

▲ **2 eggs**
  60g lean shaved ham, fat trimmed
  2 x 40g slices soy and linseed bread
  1 tbs basil pesto

Filling & Healthy Foods are marked with a green triangle.
These foods help fill you up and keep you healthy.

1 Bring a large saucepan of water to the boil over medium-high heat. Reduce heat until water is barely simmering. Carefully break 1 egg into a cup, then slide egg into water. Repeat with remaining egg. Poach eggs gently for 1-2 minutes or until egg whites are set and yolks are still soft.

2 Meanwhile, lightly spray a medium non-stick frying pan with oil and heat over medium heat. Add ham and cook for 1-2 minutes each side or until crisp.

3 Toast bread and place on serving plates. Top with ham, eggs and pesto. Serve.

SERVE WITH: 0 *ProPoints* value grilled roma tomatoes.

▶ **TIP**
You can make fried or scrambled eggs using oil spray instead of poached eggs. The ProPoints values remain the same.

Cheat's Danish with poached apricots

 7 **ProPoints** VALUES PER SERVE | **SERVES:** 2 | **PREP:** 5 MINS | **COOKING TIME:** 5 MINS

▲ **400g can Weight Watchers Halved Apricots**
▲ **¼ tsp ground cinnamon, plus extra to sprinkle**
 1 tsp cornflour
 2 x 60g small croissants, split (see note)
 ⅓ cup (80g) low-fat Greek-style natural yoghurt

Filling & Healthy Foods are marked with a green triangle. These foods help fill you up and keep you healthy.

1 Drain apricots, reserving ⅓ cup (80ml) juice. Cut each apricot in half and place in a small saucepan with reserved juice and cinnamon. Bring to the boil over medium heat. Blend cornflour with 2 teaspoons water in a small bowl. Gradually stir cornflour mixture into apricot mixture. Cook, stirring, for 1-2 minutes or until slightly thickened.

2 Meanwhile, toast croissants until golden. Place croissant bases on serving plates. Top with poached apricots and a dollop of yoghurt. Top with remaining croissant tops. Serve sprinkled with extra cinnamon.

NOTE: You can buy small croissants from the bakery section of most supermarkets.

▶ **TIP**
You can use reduced-fat custard instead of yoghurt. The **ProPoints** values remains the same.

Mushrooms with spinach, ham & cottage cheese

 ProPoints VALUES PER SERVE | **SERVES:** 2 | **PREP:** 10 MINS | **COOKING TIME:** 5 MINS

▲ **200g Swiss brown mushrooms, quartered**
▲ **1 garlic clove, crushed**
▲ **80g 97% fat-free ham, chopped**
▲ **2½ cups (75g) baby spinach leaves**
  1 tsp balsamic vinegar
  2 x 40g slices soy and linseed bread
▲ **¼ cup (60g) Weight Watchers Cottage Cheese**

Filling & Healthy Foods are marked with a green triangle.
These foods help fill you up and keep you healthy.

1 Lightly spray a large non-stick frying pan with oil and heat over medium-high heat. Add mushrooms and cook, stirring, for 3-4 minutes or until tender and lightly browned. Add garlic and cook, stirring, for 10 seconds. Add ham and spinach and cook, stirring, for 2 minutes or until spinach has just wilted. Add vinegar and stir to combine. Season with sea salt and freshly ground black pepper.
2 Meanwhile, toast bread and spread with cottage cheese. Serve topped with mushroom mixture.

▸ **TIP**
You can use low-fat smooth ricotta cheese instead of cottage cheese. The ProPoints values remain the same.

B.E.S.T. breakfast burger

 ProPoints VALUES PER SERVE | **SERVES:** 2 | **PREP:** 10 MINS | **COOKING TIME:** 10 MINS

1 (125g) thick lean beef sausage
▲ 4 slices (60g) Weight Watchers Bacon,
    fat trimmed
▲ 2 roma tomatoes, halved lengthways
▲ 2 eggs
    2 x 60g slices Turkish bread, split
▲ ⅔ cup (20g) baby spinach leaves
    2 tbs tomato chutney

Filling & Healthy Foods are marked with a green triangle.
These foods help fill you up and keep you healthy.

1 Lightly spray a large non-stick frying pan with oil and heat over medium-high heat. Cook sausage and bacon, turning occasionally, for 3-4 minutes or until sausage is cooked through and bacon is crisp. Slice sausage thinly. Transfer to a plate with bacon and cover to keep warm. Cook tomatoes for 1-2 minutes each side or until tender.

2 Lightly spray same cleaned pan with oil and heat over medium heat. Pan-fry eggs for 3 minutes or until cooked to your liking.

3 Toast bread on both sides. Top each base with spinach, tomato, sausage, bacon, egg and chutney. Sandwich with bread tops and serve.

SERVE WITH: 0 **ProPoints** value steamed asparagus, plus 200g button mushrooms (sliced) pan-fried in 1 teaspoon olive oil. Add 1 **ProPoints** value per serve for mushrooms.

Raspberry hotcakes

 ProPoints VALUES PER SERVE | **SERVES:** 4 | **PREP:** 10 MINS | **COOKING TIME:** 10 MINS

½ cup (80g) wholemeal self-raising flour
½ cup (75g) self-raising flour
1 tsp baking powder
2 tsp caster sugar
½ cup (125ml) reduced-fat milk
▲ 2 eggs
1 tsp vanilla essence
▲ 150g fresh raspberries, plus extra to garnish
200g low-fat vanilla yoghurt
2 tbs maple syrup

Filling & Healthy Foods are marked with a green triangle.
These foods help fill you up and keep you healthy.

1 Sift flours and baking powder into a medium bowl. Return husks to bowl. Stir in sugar. Whisk milk, eggs and vanilla in a jug until combined. Make a well in centre of flour mixture. Add egg mixture and whisk until smooth. Gently fold in raspberries.
2 Lightly spray a large non-stick frying pan with oil and heat over medium heat. Drop 2 heaped tablespoons of batter into pan and gently spread to make a 10cm hotcake. Cook for 1-2 minutes or until bubbles rise to the surface. Turn and cook for 1-2 minutes or until hotcake is lightly browned (see note). Transfer to a plate and cover to keep warm. Repeat with remaining batter to make 8 hotcakes.
3 Top hotcakes with a dollop of yoghurt and drizzle with maple syrup. Serve with extra raspberries.
NOTE: You can cook 2-3 hotcakes at a time in a large pan. Ensure the heat is not too high or the hotcakes will brown too quickly but won't be cooked all the way through.

▶ **TIP**
You can use fresh blueberries or pear or apple (chopped) instead of raspberries. The **ProPoints** values remain the same.

IT TAKES LESS THAN 30 MINUTES TO WHIP UP THESE LIGHT AND FLUFFY HOTCAKES DRIZZLED WITH MAPLE SYRUP. WHAT A DELICIOUS WAY TO START YOUR DAY!

Persian eggs with feta & sumac

 7 ProPoints VALUES PER SERVE | **SERVES:** 2 | **PREP:** 10 MINS | **COOKING TIME:** 30 MINS

- ▲ **1 brown onion, finely chopped**
- ▲ **1 celery stick, finely chopped**
- ▲ **1 small red capsicum, finely chopped**
- ▲ **1 tsp ground cumin**
- ▲ **400g can diced tomatoes**
- ▲ **½ cup (40g) drained canned chickpeas**
- ▲ **2 eggs**
  30g drained Persian feta cheese, crumbled
- ▲ **¼ tsp sumac (see note)**
- ▲ **¼ cup coarsely chopped fresh mint leaves**
  1 x 70g wholemeal Lebanese bread, torn

Filling & Healthy Foods are marked with a green triangle.
These foods help fill you up and keep you healthy.

1 Lightly spray a medium non-stick frying pan with oil and heat over medium heat. Add onion, celery and capsicum and cook, stirring, for 3-4 minutes or until softened. Add cumin and cook, stirring, for 1 minute or until fragrant.

2 Add tomatoes and 1 cup (250ml) water and bring to the boil. Reduce heat and simmer, uncovered, for 20 minutes or until slightly thickened. Stir in chickpeas. Season with salt and freshly ground black pepper.

3 Using a large spoon, make 2 indentations in the tomato mixture. Gently break an egg into each indentation. Cover and cook over medium heat for 3 minutes or until egg whites are set and yolks remain soft. Spoon tomato mixture and eggs onto serving plates. Sprinkle with feta, sumac and mint. Serve with Lebanese bread.

NOTE: Sumac is a purple-red coloured spice with a tart, lemony flavour often used in Middle Eastern food. Find it in the spice aisle of most supermarkets.

▶ TIP

The tomato and chickpea mixture can be made up to 3 days ahead. Store in an airtight container in the fridge.

Quinoa bircher muesli

 7 ProPoints VALUES PER SERVE | **SERVES:** 2 | **PREP:** 15 MINS | **COOKING TIME:** 10 MINS, PLUS 20 MINS STANDING

▲ ¼ cup (50g) quinoa, rinsed, drained (see note)
▲ ½ cup (45g) traditional rolled oats
   1 tbs pepitas (pumpkin seed kernels)
▲ 1 green apple, unpeeled, grated
   ½ cup (125ml) no-added-sugar apple juice
▲ ½ cup (140g) no-fat Greek-style natural
     yoghurt
▲ 30g fresh blueberries

Filling & Healthy Foods are marked with a green triangle.
These foods help fill you up and keep you healthy.

1 Bring ⅔ cup (160ml) water to the boil in a small
saucepan over high heat. Add quinoa. Reduce heat
and simmer, covered, for 8-10 minutes or until
water has absorbed. Drain and cool.
2 Place quinoa, oats, pepitas, apple, juice and
yoghurt in a large bowl. Cover and set aside for
20 minutes.
3 Serve muesli topped with blueberries.
NOTE: Quinoa (say "keen-wah") is a tiny seed
that has a slightly nutty flavour and fluffy texture
when cooked. It is a good substitute for rice. Find
it in the health-food section of most supermarkets
or from health-food stores.

French toast 2 ways

SAVOURY:
ProPoints VALUES PER SERVE | **SERVES:** 2
PREP: 15 MINS | **COOKING TIME:** 15 MINS

SWEET:
ProPoints VALUES PER SERVE | **SERVES:** 2
PREP: 15 MINS | **COOKING TIME:** 15 MINS

▲ **2 eggs**
▲ **⅓ cup (80ml) skim milk**
▲ **4 x 40g slices crusty dark rye bread**

SAVOURY TOPPING
▲ **2 slices (30g) Weight Watchers Bacon, fat trimmed, cut into strips**
▲ **200g tomato medley (a mix of red and yellow grape tomatoes), halved**
▲ **¼ cup coarsely chopped fresh flat-leaf parsley leaves**
  2 tsp slivered almonds, toasted (see tip)
▲ **1 tbs lemon juice**

SWEET TOPPING
▲ **125g fresh strawberries, halved**
  1 tsp vanilla extract
  2 tbs maple syrup

Filling & Healthy Foods are marked with a green triangle.
These foods help fill you up and keep you healthy.

1 Whisk eggs and milk in a medium bowl. Lightly spray a large non-stick frying pan with oil and heat over medium heat. Dip bread, 1 slice at a time, into egg mixture for 30 seconds or until well coated. Cook for 1-2 minutes each side or until golden brown. Serve French toast with topping of your choice (see below - each topping makes enough for 4 pieces of toast):

SAVOURY TOPPING: Lightly spray a large non-stick frying pan with oil and heat over medium-high heat. Cook bacon and tomatoes, stirring occasionally, for 5 minutes or until bacon is slightly browned and tomatoes start to soften. Meanwhile, combine parsley, almonds and juice in a small bowl. Serve French toast topped with bacon, tomatoes and parsley salsa.

SWEET TOPPING: Place strawberries, vanilla and maple syrup in a small saucepan over medium heat. Bring to the boil. Reduce heat and simmer, uncovered, for 2-3 minutes or until strawberries are just soft. Serve French toast topped with strawberry mixture.

▶ **TIP**
To toast almonds, preheat oven to 200°C or 180°C fan-forced. Spread almonds on a baking tray and bake for 4–5 minutes or until lightly toasted.

10 Simple breakfast ideas

1 Bacon & egg muffin

 ProPoints VALUES PER SERVE | **SERVES:** 1

Top **1 wholemeal English muffin** (split, toasted) with △ **1 egg** (poached), △ **2 slices Weight Watchers Bacon** (fat trimmed, grilled), **2 tsp tomato sauce** and △ **½ cup baby rocket leaves**. Serve.

2 Breakfast bean burrito

 ProPoints VALUES PER SERVE | **SERVES:** 1

Top **1 x 40g multigrain tortilla** with a **130g can Weight Watchers Baked Beans** (warmed), △ **1 small tomato** (chopped), **1 tbs Bega So Extra Light grated tasty cheese** and △ **1 cup baby spinach leaves**. Roll to enclose filling and toast in a preheated sandwich press for 2 minutes. Serve.

3 Spinach & ricotta omelette

 ProPoints VALUES PER SERVE | **SERVES:** 1

Heat **1 tsp olive oil** in a non-stick frying pan over high heat. Add △ **1 cup baby spinach leaves** and cook, stirring, until just wilted. Pour over △ **2 eggs** (lightly beaten) and sprinkle with **1 tbs reduced-fat fresh ricotta cheese**. Cook for 1-2 minutes or until almost set. Fold in half and serve with **1 x 35g slice soy & linseed toast** spread with **1 tsp Weight Watchers Canola Spread**.

4 Grilled cheesy mushroom & tomato on toast

 ProPoints VALUES PER SERVE | **SERVES:** 1

Preheat grill on high. Grill △ **1 large field mushroom** and △ **1 tomato** (halved) until slightly tender. Top mushroom with **1 slice reduced-fat Swiss cheese**. Grill until cheese has melted and tomatoes are cooked. Place on **1 x 35g slice wholemeal toast** and top with △ **1 cup baby rocket leaves** drizzled with **1 tsp olive oil**. Serve.

5 Egg, avocado & dukkah on rye

 ProPoints VALUES PER SERVE | **SERVES:** 1

Heat **1 tsp canola oil** in a small non-stick frying pan. Pan-fry △ **1 egg** until cooked to your liking. Place on △ **1 x 40g slice dark rye toast** with **¼ medium avocado** (sliced) sprinkled with **1 tsp dukkah**. Serve with △ **6 cherry tomatoes** (halved).

NOTE: Dukkah is a mix of nuts, seeds and spices used in Middle Eastern cooking. Find it in the spice aisle of most supermarkets.

6 Plum & almond crumpets

 ProPoints VALUES PER SERVE | **SERVES:** 1

Preheat grill on high. Grill △ **2 plums** (halved, stone removed), cut-side up, until soft. Top **2 wholemeal crumpets** (toasted) with plums, △ **¼ cup Weight Watchers Cottage Cheese** and **6 almonds** (chopped). Serve.

7 Pear, pecan & coconut porridge

 ProPoints VALUES PER SERVE | **SERVES:** 1

Combine ▲ **⅓ cup traditional rolled oats** with ▲ **1 cup skim milk**, ▲ **½ pear** (chopped), **5 pecans** (chopped) and **1 tbs shredded coconut** in a small saucepan. Cook, stirring, over medium heat until oats are soft and creamy. Serve with remaining ▲ **½ pear** (chopped) drizzled with **1 tsp maple syrup**.

8 Banana & walnut cereal biscuits

 ProPoints VALUES PER SERVE | **SERVES:** 1

Top ▲ **2 cereal wheat biscuits** with ▲ **⅔ cup skim milk** (warmed), ▲ **1 small banana** (sliced), ▲ **2 tbs low-fat natural yoghurt** and **1 tbs chopped walnuts**. Serve.

9 Strawberry yoghurt with muesli crunch

 ProPoints VALUES PER SERVE | **SERVES:** 1

Combine ▲ **1 cup chopped fresh strawberries** and ▲ **150g tub Nestlé Soleil Strawberry Yoghurt** in a small bowl. Mix together **2 tbs toasted muesli** and **1 tbs ground LSA mix** or **almond meal**. Sprinkle yoghurt mixture with muesli mixture and drizzle with **1 tsp honey**. Serve.

NOTE: LSA mix is a blend of ground linseeds, sunflower seeds and almonds. Find it in the health-food section of most supermarkets and store it in the fridge.

10 Ricotta, peach & cinnamon raisin toast

 ProPoints VALUES PER SERVE | **SERVES:** 1

Spread **1 x 65g slice café-style raisin toast** with **¼ cup reduced-fat fresh ricotta cheese** and top with ▲ **1 peach** (thinly sliced). Serve sprinkled with ▲ **½ tsp ground cinnamon**.

LIFT LUNCH TO
NEW FLAVOUR
HEIGHTS WITH THIS
DELICIOUSLY
SIMPLE SELECTION
OF MIDDAY MEALS.

Fresh & filling
LUNCHES

Haloumi, brown rice & spinach salad

 ProPoints VALUES PER SERVE | **SERVES:** 2 | **PREP:** 15 MINS | **COOKING TIME:** 15 MINS

2 tsp olive oil
▲ **1 garlic clove, crushed**
▲ **1 red capsicum, chopped**
▲ **2 field mushrooms**
▲ **150g cherry tomatoes**
100g haloumi cheese, thinly sliced
250g pkt microwave 90-second brown rice
▲ **2½ cups (75g) baby spinach leaves**
▲ **2 tbs lemon juice**

Filling & Healthy Foods are marked with a green triangle.
These foods help fill you up and keep you healthy.

1 Preheat a barbecue or chargrill over high heat. Combine oil and garlic in a small bowl. Drizzle or brush oil mixture over capsicum, mushrooms and tomatoes. Cook vegetables, in batches, for 5-6 minutes or until lightly charred and tender. Thickly slice mushrooms. Place vegetables in a large bowl.
2 Grill haloumi for 1 minute each side or until golden. Heat rice following packet instructions.
3 Add spinach, juice and rice to grilled vegetables and toss gently to combine. Serve rice salad topped with grilled haloumi.

▶ **TIP**
*You can use 250g cooked brown rice instead of microwave 90-second brown rice. The recipe will then have 8 **ProPoints** values per serve.*

Tuna & spinach tarts

 ProPoints VALUES PER TART | **MAKES:** 6 | **PREP:** 20 MINS | **COOKING TIME:** 30 MINS

6 x 37g slices wholegrain bread,
   crusts removed

2 tsp olive oil

▲ 3 green shallots, thinly sliced

▲ 3 cups (90g) baby spinach leaves

▲ 3 eggs

▲ 185g can tuna in springwater, drained, flaked

▲ 1 tbs chopped fresh dill leaves

⅓ cup (40g) Bega So Extra Light grated
   tasty cheese

Filling & Healthy Foods are marked with a green triangle.
These foods help fill you up and keep you healthy.

1 Preheat oven to 200°C or 180°C fan-forced. Lightly spray six ¾-cup/185ml capacity Texas muffin tin holes with oil. Using a rolling pin, roll bread slices until 3mm thick and lightly spray with oil. Line prepared tin holes with bread cases. Bake for 12 minutes or until golden and crisp. Transfer to a wire rack to cool. Return bread cases to tin holes. Reduce oven to 180°C or 160°C fan-forced.

2 Meanwhile, heat oil in a medium non-stick frying pan over medium heat. Add shallots and cook, stirring, for 3-4 minutes or until softened. Add spinach and cook, stirring, for 1 minute or until wilted. Transfer to a large bowl. Cool.

3 Lightly whisk eggs in a jug until combined. Season with salt and freshly ground black pepper. Combine spinach mixture, tuna, dill and half the cheese in a medium bowl.

4 Divide spinach mixture evenly between bread cases. Pour in egg and sprinkle with remaining cheese. Bake for 15-20 minutes or until golden and filling is just set. Serve.

SERVE WITH: 0 **ProPoints** value salad of red onion (finely chopped) and red and yellow grape tomatoes (halved), drizzled with balsamic vinegar.

▶ **TIP**
You can use canned pink or red salmon instead of tuna. The **ProPoints** values remain the same.

Prawn, cucumber & watercress baguette

 ProPoints VALUES PER SERVE | **SERVES:** 2 | **PREP:** 15 MINS

1½ tbs low-fat whole-egg mayonnaise
▲ ½ tsp finely grated lime rind
▲ 2 tsp lime juice
▲ 1 small fresh red birdseye chilli, deseeded, finely chopped
2 x 100g pieces baguette, split
▲ 25g watercress
▲ 1 Lebanese cucumber, cut into thin ribbons (see note)
▲ 150g cooked peeled prawns

Filling & Healthy Foods are marked with a green triangle. These foods help fill you up and keep you healthy.

1 Combine mayonnaise, rind, juice and chilli in a small bowl. Season with salt and freshly ground black pepper.
2 Place baguette bases on serving plates. Spread with half the mayonnaise mixture. Top with watercress, cucumber and prawns. Dollop with remaining mayonnaise mixture and sandwich with baguette tops. Serve.
NOTE: Use a vegetable peeler to cut cucumber into thin ribbons.

▶ **TIP**
You can use 100g sliced smoked salmon instead of prawns. The recipe will then have 12 ProPoints values per serve.

ENJOY A CRUSTY BREAD ROLL, PLUMP PINK PRAWNS AND CREAMY MAYO LACED WITH LIME AND CHILLI.

Poached salmon with asparagus & puy lentils

 ProPoints VALUES PER SERVE | **SERVES:** 2 | **PREP:** 15 MINS | **COOKING TIME:** 25 MINS

200g skinless salmon fillet
▲ **¼ cup (50g) dried puy lentils (see note)**
▲ **½ cup (60g) frozen peas**
▲ **1 bunch asparagus, halved**
▲ **1 celery stick, finely chopped**
▲ **30g watercress**
▲ **2 tsp finely chopped fresh dill**
  2 tsp olive oil
  1 tsp white wine vinegar
▲ **1 tbs lemon juice**

Filling & Healthy Foods are marked with a green triangle. These foods help fill you up and keep you healthy.

1 Place salmon in a large saucepan of cold water over medium heat. Bring to the boil. Reduce heat and simmer, uncovered, for 2–3 minutes. Remove from heat. Cover and set aside for 2–3 minutes or until salmon is almost cooked through. Using a fork, break salmon into large flakes. Discard any dark flesh.

2 Meanwhile, add lentils to a small saucepan of boiling water. Reduce heat and simmer for 20 minutes or until softened. Drain.

3 Boil, steam or microwave peas and asparagus, until just tender. Drain. Refresh under cold water. Pat dry with paper towels.

4 Combine celery, watercress, dill, salmon, lentils, peas and asparagus in a large bowl. Whisk oil, vinegar and juice in a small bowl. Season with salt and freshly ground black pepper. Add dressing to salad and toss gently to combine. Serve.

NOTE: Puy lentils (also known as French-style lentils) are small dark green lentils. Find them in the dried beans aisle of most supermarkets. You can use a 400g can of brown lentils (rinsed, drained) instead of puy lentils. The recipe will then have 10 **ProPoints** values per serve.

▶ **TIP**
Instead of poaching the salmon you can grill it on 1 side only for 5–7 minutes or until golden and almost cooked through.

Corn chowder with rye

 ProPoints VALUES PER SERVE | **SERVES:** 2 | **PREP:** 10 MINS | **COOKING TIME:** 30 MINS | SUITABLE TO FREEZE

2 tsp olive oil
▲ **½ small red capsicum, chopped**
▲ **1 brown onion, finely chopped**
▲ **1 celery stick, finely chopped**
▲ **2 ½ cups (400g) frozen corn kernels (see tip)**
 ½ tsp Cajun seasoning
 2 cups (500ml) reduced-salt chicken stock
▲ **3 fresh thyme sprigs**
 2 x 40g slices rye bread
▲ **2 tbs Weight Watchers Cottage Cheese**

Filling & Healthy Foods are marked with a green triangle.
These foods help fill you up and keep you healthy.

1 Heat half the oil in a large saucepan over medium heat. Add capsicum and cook, stirring, for 2-3 minutes or until softened. Transfer to a plate and set aside. Heat remaining oil in same pan over medium heat. Add onion and celery and cook, stirring, for 3-4 minutes or until softened.
2 Add corn and seasoning and cook for 1 minute. Add stock, ½ cup (125ml) water and 1 thyme sprig and bring to the boil. Reduce heat and simmer, covered, for 20 minutes. Set aside to cool slightly. Remove and discard thyme.
3 Transfer 2 cups (500ml) soup to a food processor or blender. Process until smooth. Return to pan with capsicum and stir chowder to combine. Season with salt and freshly ground black pepper.
4 Toast bread. Spread toast with cottage cheese and sprinkle with leaves from remaining thyme sprigs. Cut in half and serve with chowder.
NOTE: Soup suitable to freeze for up to 3 months.

▶**TIP**
*You can use fresh or canned corn kernels instead of frozen corn. The **ProPoints** values remain the same with fresh kernels and will have 10 **ProPoints** values per serve with canned.*

Roast beef, beetroot & feta salad

 ProPoints VALUES PER SERVE | **SERVES:** 2 | **PREP:** 20 MINS | **COOKING TIME:** 40 MINS

▲ **3 small beetroots, peeled, quartered
    (see note)**
▲ **1 red onion, cut into thin wedges**
▲ **300g Kent pumpkin, cut into thin wedges**
▲ **2 tsp lemon juice**
   3 tsp Dijon mustard
   2 tbs 97% fat-free mayonnaise
▲ **¼ cup finely chopped fresh chives**
▲ **2 cups (60g) mixed salad leaves**
   **100g thinly sliced lean deli or leftover roast
      beef, fat trimmed**
   30g reduced-fat feta cheese, crumbled
   1 tbs walnuts, coarsely chopped

Filling & Healthy Foods are marked with a green triangle.
These foods help fill you up and keep you healthy.

1 Preheat oven to 200°C or 180°C fan-forced. Line a large baking tray with baking paper. Place beetroot, onion and pumpkin on a large baking tray. Lightly spray with oil and season with salt and freshly ground black pepper. Bake for 40 minutes or until tender. Transfer to a large bowl.

2 Meanwhile, whisk juice, mustard, mayonnaise and 2 teaspoons warm water in a small bowl. Stir in half the chives.

3 Add salad leaves, beef, feta and walnuts to roasted vegetables and toss gently to combine. Drizzle salad with dressing and serve sprinkled with remaining chives.

NOTE: Wear disposable gloves when peeling beetroot so it doesn't stain your hands.

▶ **TIP**
*This recipe can be made with any leftover roast meat, such as lean lamb, chicken or pork. The **ProPoints** values remain the same with lamb and will be 6 **ProPoints** values per serve with chicken or pork.*

PLAN AHEAD AND COOK THE BEETROOT AND
PUMPKIN WITH YOUR SUNDAY ROAST. WARM THEM
IN THE MICROWAVE BEFORE TOSSING TOGETHER THIS
SATISFYING SALAD USING THE LEFTOVER MEAT.

Toasted rye with spicy avocado, salmon & snow pea shoots

 ProPoints VALUES PER SERVE | **SERVES:** 2 | **PREP:** 10 MINS | **COOKING TIME:** 5 MINS

½ medium avocado
▲ 1 tbs chopped fresh chives
▲ 1 tsp lime juice
▲ Pinch dried red chilli flakes
▲ 2 x 40g slices dark rye bread
▲ ¾ Lebanese cucumber, thinly sliced
150g sliced smoked salmon
▲ 20g snow pea shoots

Filling & Healthy Foods are marked with a green triangle.
These foods help fill you up and keep you healthy.

1 Combine avocado, chives, juice and chilli in a small bowl. Mash with a fork until almost smooth. Season with salt and freshly ground black pepper.
2 Toast bread. Spread toast with avocado mixture. Serve topped with cucumber, salmon and snow pea shoots.
SERVE WITH: O **ProPoints** value salad of baby spinach leaves and cherry tomatoes.

▶ **TIP**
*You can use watercress instead of snow pea shoots. The **ProPoints** values remain the same.*

PILED HIGH WITH SLICES OF SUCCULENT
SMOKED SALMON ON A LAYER OF
CREAMY AVOCADO, THIS GOURMET
SANDWICH IS FRESH AND FABULOUS.

Satay egg & chicken salad wrap

 ProPoints VALUES PER SERVE | **SERVES:** 2 | **PREP:** 10 MINS

▲ **2 hard-boiled eggs (see note)**
▲ **1 tbs low-fat natural yoghurt**
  ¼ tsp curry powder
  1 tbs reduced-fat smooth peanut butter
  2 x 40g soft wholegrain wraps
▲ **4 butter lettuce leaves**
▲ **100g skinless lean cooked chicken breast,**
  shredded
▲ **1 carrot, grated**
▲ **30g snow pea sprouts**

Filling & Healthy Foods are marked with a green triangle.
These foods help fill you up and keep you healthy.

1 Place eggs in a small bowl and mash with a
fork. Add yoghurt and curry powder and season
with salt and freshly ground black pepper. Stir
to combine.
2 Spread peanut butter over wraps. Top with egg
mixture, lettuce, chicken, carrot and snow pea
sprouts. Roll to enclose filling. Cut in half to serve.
NOTE: To cook hard-boiled eggs, place room-
temperature eggs in a small saucepan of water and
bring to the boil. Boil for 8-10 minutes. Drain and
run under cold water until eggs have cooled.

▶ **TIP**
*You can use 100g thinly sliced lean
deli rare roast beef (fat trimmed)
instead of chicken. The* **ProPoints**
values remain the same.

Couscous salad with tuna, tomatoes, olives & rocket

 ProPoints VALUES PER SERVE | **SERVES:** 2 | **PREP:** 5 MINS | **COOKING TIME:** 5 MINS

½ cup (90g) couscous
▲ 185g can tuna in springwater, drained, flaked
¼ cup (40g) pitted kalamata olives, sliced
▲ 2 vine-ripened tomatoes, chopped
▲ 2½ cups (75g) baby rocket leaves
1 tbs balsamic vinegar
2 tsp olive oil

Filling & Healthy Foods are marked with a green triangle.
These foods help fill you up and keep you healthy.

1 Place couscous in a large heatproof bowl. Add
½ cup (125ml) boiling water. Stir, cover and set
aside for 5 minutes or until liquid has absorbed.
Scrape with a fork to separate the grains.
2 Add tuna, olives, tomatoes, rocket, vinegar and
oil and toss to combine. Season with salt and
freshly ground black pepper. Serve.

▶ **TIP**
*You can use canned pink salmon
instead of tuna. The **ProPoints**
values remain the same.*

Spiced rice & chickpea soup

 ProPoints VALUES PER SERVE | **SERVES:** 2 | **PREP:** 15 MINS | **COOKING TIME:** 30 MINS | SUITABLE TO FREEZE

1 tbs olive oil
▲ **1 brown onion, finely chopped**
▲ **2 tsp finely grated fresh ginger**
▲ **1 garlic clove, crushed**
2 tsp garam masala (see tip)
2 cups (500ml) vegetable stock
▲ **1 carrot, cut into 1cm pieces**
▲ **200g canned chickpeas, rinsed, drained**
¼ cup (50g) long-grain white rice
▲ **¼ cup (30g) frozen peas**
▲ **50g green beans, chopped**
▲ **2 tbs no-fat Greek-style natural yoghurt**
▲ **Coriander sprigs**

Filling & Healthy Foods are marked with a green triangle.
These foods help fill you up and keep you healthy.

1 Heat oil in a medium saucepan over medium-high heat. Cook onion, ginger, garlic and garam masala, stirring, for 4-5 minutes or until onion has softened.
2 Add stock, 1 cup (250ml) water, carrot, chickpeas and rice. Bring to the boil. Reduce heat and simmer, uncovered, for 15 minutes or until rice is just tender.
3 Add peas and beans and simmer, uncovered, for 5 minutes or until beans are tender. Serve soup topped with yoghurt and coriander.
NOTE: Soup suitable to freeze (without toppings) for up to 3 months.

▶ **TIP**

Used in Indian cooking, garam masala is a ground spice blend that usually includes pepper, caraway seeds, fennel seeds, cardamom, cinnamon and cloves. Find it in the spice aisle of most supermarkets.

AS YOU INHALE THE AROMATIC SPICES
IN THIS EXOTIC SOUP YOU'LL BE TRANSPORTED
FAR AWAY FROM THE OFFICE AND UNFINISHED
CHORES – AT LEAST UNTIL LUNCHTIME IS OVER!

Asian-style soup with tofu

 ProPoints VALUES PER SERVE | **SERVES:** 2 | **PREP:** 15 MINS | **COOKING TIME:** 10 MINS

20g sachet instant miso soup (see note)
2 cups (500ml) reduced-salt chicken stock
2 tsp soy sauce
▲ 1 carrot, cut into matchsticks
▲ 25g snow peas, thinly sliced
30g rice vermicelli noodles
▲ 1 cup (30g) baby spinach leaves
▲ 70g firm tofu, cut into 1cm pieces

Filling & Healthy Foods are marked with a green triangle.
These foods help fill you up and keep you healthy.

1 Whisk miso, stock and soy sauce in a small
saucepan over medium heat until combined.
Bring to the boil. Reduce heat and simmer,
uncovered, for 5 minutes.
2 Add carrot, snow peas and noodles to stock
mixture and bring to the boil. Reduce heat and
simmer, uncovered, for 2 minutes or until noodles
are tender. Stir in spinach and tofu. Serve.
NOTE: Popular in Japanese soups and stews, miso
paste is made from fermented soy beans. Instant
miso soup is a powdered form of this salty paste.
Find it in the Asian section of most supermarkets
or from Asian grocery stores. You can use a
vegetable stock cube instead of instant miso soup.

▶ TIP
*You can add 150g peeled green
prawns with the noodles in
Step 2. Add 1 ProPoints value
per serve.*

Chicken & eggplant pita pockets

 ProPoints VALUES PER SERVE | **SERVES:** 2 | **PREP:** 10 MINS

▲ **1 carrot, grated**
   2 tsp currants
▲ **1 tbs finely chopped fresh flat-leaf parsley**
   40g reduced-fat feta cheese, crumbled
▲ **1 tbs lemon juice**
   2 x 45g lite wholemeal pita pockets, warmed
   ¼ cup (60g) ready-made eggplant dip
▲ **1 small zucchini, grated**
▲ **150g skinless lean cooked chicken breast, shredded**

Filling & Healthy Foods are marked with a green triangle.
These foods help fill you up and keep you healthy.

1 Combine carrot, currants, parsley, feta and juice in a medium bowl.
2 Cut each pita pocket in half. Carefully open pocket and fill with eggplant dip, zucchini, chicken and carrot mixture. Serve.

▶ **TIP**
You can use a 185g can tuna in springwater (drained, flaked) instead of chicken. The ProPoints values remain the same.

Pasta with sweet potato & goat's cheese

 ProPoints VALUES PER SERVE | **SERVES:** 4 | **PREP:** 20 MINS | **COOKING TIME:** 35 MINS, PLUS COOLING

△ **300g sweet potato (kumara), cut into**
  2cm pieces
△ **200g wholemeal spiral pasta**
△ **400g can red kidney beans, rinsed, drained**
△ **150g yellow grape tomatoes, halved**
△ **2 cups (60g) baby rocket leaves**
  80g goat's cheese, crumbled
  1 tbs extra-virgin olive oil
△ **1 tbs lemon juice**
△ **1 tbs finely chopped fresh flat-leaf parsley**
△ **1 garlic clove, crushed**

Filling & Healthy Foods are marked with a green triangle.
These foods help fill you up and keep you healthy.

1 Preheat oven to 200°C or 180°C fan-forced.
Line a baking tray with baking paper. Place sweet
potato on prepared tray and lightly spray with oil.
Bake for 35-40 minutes or until golden and tender.
Cool slightly.
2 Meanwhile, cook pasta in a large saucepan of
boiling salted water, following packet instructions,
or until just tender. Drain and rinse under cold
water. Drain well. Combine beans, tomatoes, rocket,
cheese, sweet potato and pasta in a large bowl.
3 Whisk oil, juice, parsley and garlic in a small bowl.
Season with salt and freshly ground black pepper.
Add dressing to salad and toss gently to combine.
Serve.

▶**TIP**

*The sweet potato can be
roasted a day ahead. Store in
an airtight container in the
fridge until required.*

Pork rice paper rolls

 ProPoints VALUES PER ROLL | **MAKES:** 8 | **PREP:** 25 MINS | **COOKING TIME:** 5 MINS

▲ **300g lean pork fillet, fat trimmed,**
   thinly sliced
▲ **2 green shallots, thinly sliced**
▲ **1 garlic clove, crushed**
   2 tbs fish sauce
   2 tbs honey
   100g rice vermicelli noodles (see note)
   8 x 22cm round rice paper sheets
▲ **½ Lebanese cucumber, cut into matchsticks**
▲ **½ carrot, cut into matchsticks**
▲ **40g snow pea sprouts**
▲ **8 large fresh mint leaves**

Filling & Healthy Foods are marked with a green triangle.
These foods help fill you up and keep you healthy.

1 Combine pork, shallots, garlic, fish sauce and
honey in a bowl and toss to coat. Preheat a large
non-stick frying pan over medium-high heat.
Cook pork for 2-3 minutes each side or until cooked
to your liking. Transfer to a plate.

2 Meanwhile, prepare noodles following packet
instructions or until just tender. Rinse under
cold water. Drain. Using scissors, cut noodles into
5cm lengths.

3 Working with 1 sheet at a time, soak rice paper in
a bowl of warm water for 10-20 seconds or until just
softened. Place on a clean tea towel to absorb
excess water. Place one-eighth of noodles along
centre of rice paper. Top with one-eighth of pork,
cucumber, carrot, sprouts and a mint leaf. Fold over
2 opposite edges of rice paper, then roll to enclose
filling. Place on a plate and cover with a slightly
damp clean tea towel to stop it drying out. Repeat
with remaining rice paper, noodles, pork, cucumber,
carrot, sprouts and mint to make 8 rolls. Serve.

NOTE: Sold in bunches, rice vermicelli noodles are
very thin noodles made from rice. Find them in the
noodle aisle of most supermarkets.

▶ **TIP**
*You can use lean chicken breast
fillet (cooked all the way
through) instead of pork fillet.
The **ProPoints** values remain
the same.*

Asian turkey sandwich

 ProPoints VALUES PER SERVE | **SERVES:** 2 | **PREP:** 10 MINS

2 tsp hoisin sauce

2 tbs low-fat mayonnaise

4 x 40g slices soy and linseed bread

▲ 150g thinly sliced 97% fat-free deli or
    leftover cooked turkey breast, fat trimmed

▲ ½ cup (90g) grated zucchini

▲ ½ cup (20g) alfalfa sprouts

Filling & Healthy Foods are marked with a green triangle.
These foods help fill you up and keep you healthy.

1 Combine hoisin sauce and mayonnaise in a small bowl. Season with salt and freshly ground black pepper.

2 Spread bread with mayonnaise mixture. Top half the bread slices with turkey, zucchini and alfalfa. Season with sea salt and freshly ground black pepper. Sandwich with remaining bread slices. Serve.

SERVE WITH: 0 **ProPoints** value carrot, celery and red capsicum sticks.

▶ **TIP**

You can use sweet chilli sauce and 1 teaspoon lime juice with the mayonnaise instead of hoisin. The recipe will then have 9 ProPoints values per serve.

NEED A LITTLE LUNCHTIME INSPIRATION? WHY NOT TRY THE UNEXPECTED BY GIVING A SIMPLE SANDWICH AN ASIAN TWIST AND USING GRATED ZUCCHINI INSTEAD OF LETTUCE.

10 Simple lunch ideas

1 Warm lentil & feta salad

 ProPoints VALUES PER SERVE | **SERVES:** 1

Place **1 tsp olive oil**, ▲ **½ cup drained canned lentils**,
▲ **1 cup baby spinach leaves**, ▲ **½ red capsicum** (chopped),
▲ **¼ red onion** (thinly sliced) and ▲ **6 grape tomatoes** in a small
saucepan over low heat. Stir until warmed through. Stir in
2 tsp balsamic vinegar and **30g reduced-fat feta cheese**
(chopped). Sprinkle with ▲ **1 tbs chopped fresh flat-leaf parsley**
and ▲ **1 tbs chopped fresh basil**. Serve.

----

2 Salmon & cream cheese crispbreads

 ProPoints VALUES PER SERVE | **SERVES:** 1

Spread ▲ **2 wholegrain crispbreads** with **2 tbs reduced-fat cream
cheese**. Top with **2 tsp capers** (rinsed, drained), **50g sliced
smoked salmon** and ▲ **½ cup baby rocket leaves**. Serve with
▲ **4 cucumber sticks** and ▲ **3 cherry tomatoes**.

----

3 Chicken & baby corn udon soup

 ProPoints VALUES PER SERVE | **SERVES:** 1

Place **2 cups reduced-salt chicken stock**, ▲ **80g diced skinless
lean cooked chicken breast**, **100g shelf-fresh udon noodles**,
1 tsp sesame oil, **1 tbs soy sauce**, ▲ **3 fresh baby corn** (halved),
▲ **1 baby bok choy** (halved) and ▲ **3 mushrooms** (quartered) in
a medium saucepan. Bring to the boil. Reduce heat and simmer for
3-4 minutes. Sprinkle with ▲ **1 green shallot** (chopped). Serve.

4 Jacket potato with cheesy coleslaw

 ProPoints VALUES PER SERVE | **SERVES:** 1

Drizzle ▲ **300g baked jacket potato** with **1 tsp flaxseed oil** and top
with ▲ **1 cup dry coleslaw mix**, ▲ **½ green capsicum** (thinly sliced),
1 tbs extra-light sour cream and **2 tbs Bega So Extra Light grated
tasty cheese**. Serve.

----

5 Open beef & horseradish rye sandwich

 ProPoints VALUES PER SERVE | **SERVES:** 1

Spread ▲ **40g slice dark rye bread** with **2 tsp horseradish cream**.
Top with ▲ **50g thinly sliced lean deli roast beef**, **2 gherkins**
(sliced), ▲ **½ Lebanese cucumber** (cut into ribbons) and ▲ **1 cup
roughly chopped watercress**. Serve.

----

6 Mackerel & coriander brown rice salad

 ProPoints VALUES PER SERVE | **SERVES:** 1

Combine **90g drained canned mackerel in brine**, ▲ **½ cup cooked
brown rice**, ▲ **½ small red onion** (finely chopped), ▲ **½ red
capsicum** (finely chopped), ▲ **4 button mushrooms** (sliced),
▲ **5 grape tomatoes**, ▲ **2 tbs coriander leaves** and juice of
▲ **½ lemon** in a bowl. Serve.

7 Thai chicken noodle salad

 ProPoints VALUES PER SERVE | **SERVES:** 1

Combine **½ cup cooked bean thread vermicelli (cellophane) noodles**, ▲ **80g shredded skinless lean cooked chicken breast**, ▲ **½ small carrot** (grated), ▲ **½ red capsicum** (thinly sliced), ▲ **1 Lebanese cucumber** (sliced), ▲ **1 green shallot** (sliced), **1 tbs sweet chilli sauce**, **1 tsp sunflower oil** and juice of ▲ **½ lemon**. Top with **1 tbs chopped peanuts** and ▲ **1 tbs coriander leaves**. Serve.

---

8 Italian platter

 ProPoints VALUES PER SERVE | **SERVES:** 1

Arrange ▲ **3 artichoke hearts in brine** (drained), **5 olives in brine** (drained), **50g sardines in tomato sauce** and **2 (13g) slices prosciutto** (fat trimmed) on a platter. Add ▲ **1 tomato** (quartered), ▲ **1 cup rocket leaves** and drizzle with **1 tsp balsamic vinegar**. Serve with **30g slice ciabatta bread**.

---

9 Tuna & egg pasta salad

 ProPoints VALUES PER SERVE | **SERVES:** 1

Combine **½ cup cooked pasta** (any small shape), ▲ **85g can tuna in springwater** (drained, flaked), ▲ **1 hard-boiled egg** (chopped), ▲ **½ carrot** (grated), ▲ **½ red capsicum** (finely chopped), ▲ **1 green shallot** (sliced) and ▲ **1 celery stick** (sliced) in a bowl. Whisk **1 tbs light whole-egg mayonnaise**, **1 tsp Dijon mustard** and ▲ **1 tsp lemon juice** in a jug until combined. Stir into tuna salad. Serve.

10 Caprese grill

 ProPoints VALUES PER SERVE | **SERVES:** 1

Preheat grill on high. Rub **40g slice sourdough toast** with cut sides of ▲ **1 garlic clove** (halved). Top with ▲ **1 tomato** (sliced), ▲ **6 basil leaves** (shredded), **1 bocconcini cheese** (sliced) and **1 tsp pine nuts**. Grill until melted. Serve with ▲ **1 cup mixed salad leaves** drizzled with **1 tsp olive oil** and **1 tsp balsamic vinegar**.

MAKE A DINNER DATE WITH
A SIMPLE AND SATISFYING
MAIN MEAL THAT EVERYONE
CAN ENJOY.

Simple & tasty
DINNERS

Devilled lamb rumps with tomato & herb salad

 ProPoints VALUES PER SERVE | **SERVES:** 4 | **PREP:** 25 MINS | **COOKING TIME:** 25 MINS, PLUS 10 MINS RESTING

⅓ cup (110g) ready-made fruit chutney
2 tsp mild curry powder
1 tbs brown sugar
1 tbs reduced-salt soy sauce
1 tbs Worcestershire sauce
2 x 375g lean lamb rumps, fat trimmed
▲ 1 Lebanese cucumber, deseeded,
   thinly sliced (see note)
▲ 4 vine-ripened tomatoes, deseeded,
   chopped (see note)
▲ ½ red onion, thinly sliced
▲ 2 tbs lime juice
1 tbs olive oil
▲ ½ cup firmly packed fresh mint leaves
▲ ½ cup firmly packed fresh coriander leaves

Filling & Healthy Foods are marked with a green triangle.
These foods help fill you up and keep you healthy.

1 Preheat oven to 220°C or 200°C fan-forced. Line a baking tray with baking paper.
2 Combine chutney, curry powder, brown sugar, soy sauce and Worcestershire in a large bowl (see tip). Add lamb and turn to coat. Transfer lamb to prepared tray. Pour over marinade. Bake, basting occasionally, for 25 minutes or until cooked to your liking. Transfer to a plate. Cover lamb with foil and set aside to rest for 10 minutes before slicing thinly.
3 Meanwhile, combine cucumber, tomatoes, onion, juice, oil, mint and coriander in a large bowl. Toss gently to combine. Drizzle lamb with pan juices and serve with salad.

NOTE: To deseed the cucumber and tomatoes, cut them in half and use a small teaspoon to scrape out the pulp and seeds.

SERVE WITH: Baked jacket potatoes. Allow 2 **ProPoints** values per serve for a 120g potato.

▶ **TIP**
For more spice, add 1 teaspoon hot English mustard or a large pinch of cayenne pepper to marinade in Step 2.

Five-spice chicken with noodles

 ProPoints VALUES PER SERVE | **SERVES:** 4 | **PREP:** 20 MINS, PLUS 3 HOURS MARINATING
COOKING TIME: 15 MINS

2 tbs kecap manis (sweet soy sauce)
2 tbs soy sauce
2 tsp cornflour
1 tsp Chinese five-spice powder (see note)
▲ 1 tsp finely grated fresh ginger
▲ 1 garlic clove, crushed
▲ 600g lean chicken breast fillets, fat trimmed, thinly sliced
200g rice stick noodles
1 tbs canola oil
▲ 1 carrot, cut into matchsticks
▲ 1 red capsicum, thinly sliced
▲ 2 green shallots, thinly sliced
▲ 1 bunch baby bok choy, cut into 5cm lengths

Filling & Healthy Foods are marked with a green triangle.
These foods help fill you up and keep you healthy.

1 Combine kecap manis, soy sauce, cornflour, five spice, ginger and garlic in a large glass or ceramic bowl. Add chicken and turn to coat. Cover and refrigerate for 3 hours.

2 Prepare noodles following packet instructions or until just tender. Drain. Using scissors, cut noodles into 5cm lengths.

3 Drain chicken, reserving marinade. Heat a wok over high heat. Add half the oil and heat for 5 seconds. Stir-fry chicken, in batches, for 5 minutes or until browned. Transfer to a bowl. Reheat wok over high heat. Add remaining oil and heat for 5 seconds. Stir-fry carrot and capsicum for 2 minutes or until just softened. Add shallots and bok choy and stir-fry for 3-4 minutes or until vegetables are tender.

4 Return chicken to wok with noodles and reserved marinade. Stir-fry until heated through. Serve.

NOTE: Chinese five-spice powder is a ground spice blend of cinnamon, star anise, cloves, fennel seeds and pepper. Find it in the spice aisle of most supermarkets.

▶ **TIP**
You can use any dried Asian noodles instead of rice stick noodles. The ProPoints values remain the same.

A GREAT MAKE-AHEAD MEAL – JUST MARINATE THE
MEAT IN THE MORNING THEN IT WILL ONLY TAKE
15 MINUTES TO COOK WHEN YOU GET HOME!

AIOLI IS A CLASSIC FRENCH MAYONNAISE
MADE WITH GARLIC. WE'VE ADDED
SUN-DRIED TOMATOES SO THESE
BURGERS REALLY TINGLE THE TASTEBUDS.

Open beef burgers with sun-dried tomato aioli

12 **ProPoints** VALUES PER SERVE | **SERVES:** 4 | **PREP:** 15 MINS | **COOKING TIME:** 10 MINS | SUITABLE TO FREEZE

400g lean beef mince
¼ cup (15g) fresh breadcrumbs made from
    white bread
▲ **2 tbs finely chopped fresh basil leaves**
1 tbs smokey barbecue sauce
▲ **1 egg**
▲ **2 garlic cloves, crushed**
¼ cup (75g) low-fat whole-egg mayonnaise
2 tbs finely chopped 97% fat-free sun-dried
    tomatoes
▲ **1 tbs lemon juice**
½ Turkish pide loaf
▲ **1 cup (30g) baby rocket leaves**
▲ **1 Lebanese cucumber, cut into thin ribbons**
    (see tip)
▲ **100g roasted red capsicum (not in oil),**
    cut into strips
▲ **½ red onion, thinly sliced**

Filling & Healthy Foods are marked with a green triangle.
These foods help fill you up and keep you healthy.

1 Combine mince, breadcrumbs, basil, sauce,
egg and half the garlic in a medium bowl. Shape
mixture into 4 patties. Press each patty until
2cm thick.
2 Lightly spray a large non-stick frying pan with
oil and heat over medium heat. Cook patties for
4-5 minutes each side or until cooked through.
3 Meanwhile, combine mayonnaise, tomatoes,
remaining garlic, juice and 2 teaspoons hot water
in a small bowl. Set aioli aside.
4 Preheat grill on high. Split Turkish loaf in half.
Cut each half into 2 pieces. Grill cut-side of bread
until lightly toasted. Place bases on serving plates.
Spread with half the aioli. Top with rocket,
cucumber, capsicum, onion and burgers. Dollop
with remaining aioli. Serve.
NOTE: Uncooked patties suitable to freeze for up
to 1 month.

▶ **TIP**
Use a vegetable peeler to slice the
cucumber into thin ribbons.

Traditional beef cannelloni

 ProPoints VALUES PER SERVE | **SERVES:** 4 | **PREP:** 30 MINS | **COOKING TIME:** 1 HOUR 15 MINS | SUITABLE TO FREEZE

1 tbs olive oil
▲ 1 brown onion, finely chopped
▲ 2 carrots, finely chopped
▲ 1 celery stick, finely chopped
400g lean beef mince
2 tbs tomato paste
1 cup (250ml) chicken stock
▲ 2 garlic cloves, crushed
▲ ⅓ cup fresh basil leaves
700g jar tomato pasta sauce
12 (250g) fresh cannelloni sheets
⅓ cup (40g) Bega So Extra Light grated
    tasty cheese

*Filling & Healthy Foods are marked with a green triangle.
These foods help fill you up and keep you healthy.*

1 Preheat oven to 200°C or 180°C fan-forced.
Lightly spray a 20cm x 30cm ovenproof dish with
oil. Heat half the oil in a large non-stick frying pan
over medium-high heat. Add onion, carrot and
celery and cook, stirring, for 5 minutes or until
softened. Add beef and cook, breaking up any
lumps, for 5 minutes or until browned.
2 Add paste and stock and bring to the boil.
Reduce heat and simmer, covered, for 10 minutes
or until thickened. Transfer to a bowl. Cool.
3 Meanwhile, heat remaining oil in same pan over
medium heat. Add garlic and basil and cook,
stirring, for 1 minute. Add pasta sauce and 1 cup
(250ml) water and bring to the boil. Reduce heat
and simmer, uncovered, for 5 minutes or until
slightly thickened.
4 Place cannelloni sheets on a flat surface.
Divide beef mixture along centre of each sheet.
Roll to enclose filling. Spoon one-quarter of pasta
sauce mixture over base of prepared dish. Place
cannelloni, seam-side down, on top of pasta sauce
mixture in dish. Spoon remaining pasta sauce
mixture over cannelloni. Cover with foil and bake
for 30 minutes. Sprinkle with cheese and bake
for 10 minutes or until cheese is melted and
golden. Serve.
NOTE: Cooked or uncooked cannelloni suitable to
freeze for up to 2 months.
SERVE WITH: 0 *ProPoints* value rocket and
spinach salad.

Turkey chilli

 12 **ProPoints** VALUES PER SERVE | **SERVES:** 4 | **PREP:** 20 MINS | **COOKING TIME:** 35 MINS | SUITABLE TO FREEZE

▲ **1 cup (200g) brown rice**
  1 tbs olive oil
▲ **1 brown onion, finely chopped**
▲ **1 red capsicum, finely chopped**
▲ **500g lean turkey breast mince**
▲ **2 garlic cloves, crushed**
  1 tsp Mexican chilli powder
▲ **400g can diced tomatoes**
  1 cup (250ml) chicken stock
▲ **2 zucchini, cut into 1cm pieces**
▲ **310g can corn kernels, rinsed, drained**
  ⅓ cup (80g) extra-light sour cream
▲ **Coriander sprigs**

Filling & Healthy Foods are marked with a green triangle.
These foods help fill you up and keep you healthy.

1 Cook rice in a large saucepan of boiling water, following packet instructions, or until tender. Drain.
2 Meanwhile, heat oil in a large non-stick frying pan over medium heat. Add onion and capsicum and cook, stirring, for 5 minutes or until softened. Add mince and cook, breaking up any lumps, for 5 minutes or until browned. Add garlic and chilli powder and cook, stirring, for 30 seconds.
3 Stir in tomatoes, stock and zucchini and bring to the boil. Reduce heat and simmer, uncovered, for 15 minutes or until slightly thickened. Stir in corn and cook for 2 minutes or until heated through.
4 Divide rice among plates and top with turkey chilli, sour cream and coriander. Serve.
NOTE: Chilli (without toppings) suitable to freeze for up to 3 months.

▶ **TIP**
*You can use lean beef mince instead of turkey mince. The recipe will then have 13 **ProPoints** values per serve.*

Fish tacos with cabbage & coriander slaw

 9 *ProPoints* VALUES PER SERVE | **SERVES:** 4 | **PREP:** 20 MINS | **COOKING TIME:** 5 MINS

▲ ¼ small white (savoy) cabbage, finely shredded

▲ ¼ red onion, thinly sliced

▲ ¼ cup finely chopped fresh coriander leaves, plus extra sprigs to garnish

1 tbs extra-virgin olive oil

▲ 2 tbs lime juice

▲ 1 tsp finely grated lime rind

▲ ½ tsp ground cumin

▲ 400g skinless firm white fish fillets, cut into 1.5cm-thick strips (see note)

4 x 40g flour tortillas

1 small avocado, mashed

⅓ cup (80g) extra-light sour cream

▲ Lime wedges

Filling & Healthy Foods are marked with a green triangle.
These foods help fill you up and keep you healthy.

1 Combine cabbage, onion, coriander and half both the oil and juice in a large bowl. Set slaw aside.

2 Combine rind, cumin and remaining oil on a plate. Season with salt and freshly ground black pepper. Add fish and turn to coat.

3 Lightly spray a large non-stick frying pan with oil and heat over medium-high heat. Cook fish for 2 minutes each side or until cooked through. Drizzle with remaining juice.

4 Heat tortillas following packet instructions. Divide tortillas among serving plates. Spread avocado over half of each tortilla. Top with slaw, fish and sour cream. Fold to enclose filling. Serve with lime wedges and coriander sprigs.

NOTE: You can use any firm white fish fillets, such as ling, blue-eye trevalla, flathead or snapper. The *ProPoints* values remain the same.

ADD SOME MEXICAN MAGIC TO YOUR WEEKNIGHTS
WITH THESE TASTY TACOS. THE LIME AND
CORIANDER IN THE COLESLAW REALLY ZINGS!

Lamb with green olive dressing & tomato couscous

 ProPoints VALUES PER SERVE | **SERVES:** 4 | **PREP:** 20 MINS | **COOKING TIME:** 10 MINS

120g green Sicilian olives, pitted, chopped
▲ **1 celery stick, finely chopped**
▲ **½ red onion, finely chopped**
▲ **2 tbs finely chopped fresh flat-leaf parsley leaves, plus extra sprigs to garnish**
1 tbs olive oil
1 tbs red wine vinegar
▲ **2 tsp coriander seeds**
▲ **4 x 150g lean lamb leg steaks, fat trimmed**
¾ cup (150g) couscous
▲ **1 zucchini, grated**
▲ **100g snow peas, shredded**
▲ **2 green shallots, thinly sliced**
▲ **250g grape tomatoes, quartered**

Filling & Healthy Foods are marked with a green triangle. These foods help fill you up and keep you healthy.

1 Combine olives, celery, onion, parsley, oil and vinegar in a small bowl. Set dressing aside.

2 Place coriander seeds in a small non-stick frying pan and cook over medium heat for 1 minute or until fragrant. Using a mortar and pestle, lightly crush seeds. Lightly spray lamb with oil and sprinkle with crushed coriander seeds.

3 Heat a barbecue or chargrill over medium-high heat. Cook lamb for 3-4 minutes each side or until cooked to your liking. Transfer to a plate. Cover lamb with foil and set aside to rest for 5 minutes.

4 Meanwhile, place couscous in a medium heatproof bowl. Add ¾ cup (185ml) boiling water. Stir, cover and set aside for 3-5 minutes or until liquid has absorbed. Scrape with a fork to separate grains. Stir in zucchini, snow peas, shallots and tomatoes. Serve couscous with lamb, dressing and a parsley sprig.

Tuna mornay

ProPoints VALUES PER SERVE | **SERVES:** 4 | **PREP:** 20 MINS | **COOKING TIME:** 50 MINS

▲ **1 cup (200g) brown rice**
  1 tbs Weight Watchers Canola Spread
▲ **1 brown onion, finely chopped**
▲ **2 celery sticks, finely chopped**
▲ **2 garlic cloves, crushed**
  2 tbs plain flour
▲ **2 cups (500ml) skim milk**
▲ **½ cup (120g) low-fat smooth ricotta cheese**
  ½ cup (60g) Bega So Extra Light grated
    tasty cheese
▲ **1 cup (200g) fresh corn kernels (see note)**
▲ **185g can tuna in springwater, drained, flaked**
  ⅓ cup (25g) fresh breadcrumbs made from
    wholegrain bread
▲ **2 tbs chopped fresh chives**

Filling & Healthy Foods are marked with a green triangle.
These foods help fill you up and keep you healthy.

1 Preheat oven to 180°C or 160°C fan-forced.
Lightly spray a 1.5L (6-cup) capacity ovenproof
dish with oil. Cook rice in a large saucepan of
boiling water, following packet instructions, or
until just tender. Drain.
2 Meanwhile, melt spread in a large saucepan over
medium heat. Add onion and celery and cook,
stirring, for 3-4 minutes or until softened. Add
garlic and cook, stirring, for 1 minute. Add flour and
cook, stirring, for 1 minute. Gradually add milk and
whisk until smooth and combined. Bring to the
boil. Reduce heat and simmer, stirring, for
1-2 minutes or until sauce has thickened.
3 Stir ricotta and tasty cheese into sauce until
smooth. Remove from heat. Stir in corn and tuna.
Spoon rice into prepared dish and top with tuna
mixture. Sprinkle with breadcrumbs and chives.
Bake for 15-20 minutes or until breadcrumbs are
golden. Serve.
NOTE: You can use frozen or canned corn instead
of fresh. The **ProPoints** values remain the same.
SERVE WITH: 0 **ProPoints** value salad of baby
spinach leaves, baby fennel (thinly sliced) and
cherry tomatoes (halved).

Oven-baked chicken schnitzel

 ProPoints VALUES PER SERVE | **SERVES:** 4 | **PREP:** 25 MINS | **COOKING TIME:** 15 MINS

▲ ¾ cup (200g) no-fat Greek-style natural
  yoghurt
  1½ cups (150g) dried packaged multigrain
  breadcrumbs
▲ ⅓ cup finely chopped fresh herbs (see note)
▲ 4 x 150g lean chicken breast schnitzels
  (uncrumbed)
▲ 400g baby (chat) potatoes, halved
▲ 1 bunch baby carrots
▲ 1 bunch broccolini
▲ 1 bunch rocket
▲ Lemon wedges

Filling & Healthy Foods are marked with a green triangle.
These foods help fill you up and keep you healthy.

1 Preheat oven to 220°C or 200°C fan-forced. Line
a baking tray with baking paper. Place yoghurt in
a shallow bowl. Combine breadcrumbs and herbs
on a plate.
2 Dip 1 schnitzel in yoghurt, scraping off any
excess. Press schnitzel in breadcrumb mixture to
coat. Lightly spray both sides with oil and place on
prepared tray. Repeat with remaining schnitzels,
yoghurt and breadcrumb mixture. Bake for
12-15 minutes or until golden and cooked through.
3 Meanwhile, boil, steam or microwave potatoes,
carrots and broccolini, separately, until tender.
Drain. Serve schnitzels with vegetables, rocket and
lemon wedges.
NOTE: Use a mixture of fresh herbs such as chives,
parsley, basil, oregano and sage.

Red wine lamb casserole with mash

 **10** **ProPoints** VALUES PER SERVE | **SERVES:** 4 | **PREP:** 15 MINS | **COOKING TIME:** 1 HOUR 40 MINS
SUITABLE TO FREEZE

▲ **500g lean lamb leg steaks, fat trimmed,**
   cut into 3cm pieces
1 tbs plain flour
1 tbs olive oil
▲ **8 eschalots**
1 cup (250ml) reduced-salt beef stock
⅔ cup (160ml) dry red wine
▲ **7 fresh thyme sprigs**
▲ **2 fresh flat-leaf parsley sprigs**
▲ **1 fresh or dried bay leaf**
▲ **1 bunch baby carrots, peeled**
▲ **600g potatoes, unpeeled, chopped**
2 tsp Weight Watchers Canola Spread
▲ **¼ cup (60ml) skim milk**

Filling & Healthy Foods are marked with a green triangle.
These foods help fill you up and keep you healthy.

1 Place lamb in a large bowl. Sprinkle with flour and season with salt and freshly ground black pepper. Toss to coat.

2 Heat half the oil in a large flameproof casserole dish over medium-high heat. Cook lamb, turning, in batches, for 4–5 minutes or until browned. Transfer to a plate.

3 Heat remaining oil in same dish over medium heat. Add eschalots and cook, stirring, for 5 minutes or until golden. Return lamb to dish with stock, wine, 3 thyme sprigs, parsley and bay leaf and bring to the boil. Reduce heat and simmer, covered, for 45 minutes. Add carrots and ½ cup (125ml) water and simmer, covered, for 20 minutes. Remove lid and simmer for 15 minutes or until lamb is tender and sauce has slightly thickened.

4 Meanwhile, boil, steam or microwave potatoes until tender. Drain. Mash in a large bowl with spread and milk until smooth. Season with salt and freshly ground black pepper. Serve casserole with mash and a thyme sprig.

NOTE: Casserole (without mash) suitable to freeze for up to 3 months.

SERVE WITH: 0 **ProPoints** value steamed green beans and baby peas.

GOT LEFTOVERS? LUCKY YOU! STEWS AND
CASSEROLES TASTE EVEN BETTER THE NEXT DAY
BECAUSE THE FLAVOURS MELD AND INTENSIFY.

Baked salmon with cherry tomatoes, olives & capers

 11 *ProPoints* VALUES PER SERVE | **SERVES:** 4 | **PREP:** 20 MINS | **COOKING TIME:** 25 MINS

1 tbs olive oil
▲ **1 brown onion, thinly sliced**
▲ **2 garlic cloves, crushed**
1 tbs baby capers, rinsed, drained
▲ **400g cherry tomatoes, halved**
½ cup (75g) pitted kalamata olives
4 x 150g skinless salmon fillets
▲ **¼ cup finely chopped fresh flat-leaf parsley leaves**
▲ **1 tsp finely grated lemon rind**

Filling & Healthy Foods are marked with a green triangle. These foods help fill you up and keep you healthy.

1 Preheat oven to 200°C or 180°C fan-forced. Heat oil in a medium saucepan over medium-high heat. Add onion and cook, stirring, for 3-4 minutes or until softened. Add garlic and capers and cook, stirring, for 30 seconds.

2 Add tomatoes and ½ cup (125ml) water and bring to the boil. Reduce heat and simmer for 5 minutes or until tomatoes have softened. Stir in olives. Transfer mixture to a large baking dish. Top with salmon and bake for 15-20 minutes or until salmon is cooked to your liking.

3 Serve salmon and tomato mixture sprinkled with parsley and rind.

SERVE WITH: 0 *ProPoints* value steamed green beans and yellow squash.

▶ **TIP**

You can use a 400g can cherry tomatoes instead of fresh tomatoes (omit the water). The ProPoints values remain the same.

Chicken teriyaki with soba noodles

 8 **ProPoints** VALUES PER SERVE | **SERVES:** 4 | **PREP:** 15 MINS, PLUS 2 HOURS MARINATING | **COOKING TIME:** 15 MINS

⅓ cup (80ml) soy sauce

1 tbs mirin (Japanese rice wine)

▲ 1 garlic clove, crushed

1½ tbs honey

▲ 2 x 200g lean chicken breast fillets, fat trimmed, halved horizontally

▲ 180g dried soba noodles (see note)

▲ 250g snow peas, halved diagonally

▲ 1 bunch broccolini, halved, stems halved lengthways

▲ 1 bunch asparagus, halved diagonally

Filling & Healthy Foods are marked with a green triangle. These foods help fill you up and keep you healthy.

1 Combine soy sauce, mirin, garlic and 1 tablespoon honey in a small heatproof bowl. Microwave on High (100%) for 20 seconds or until warm. Stir until honey has dissolved. Place chicken in a medium glass or ceramic bowl. Add soy mixture and turn to coat. Cover and refrigerate for 2 hours.

2 Lightly spray a large non-stick frying pan with oil and heat over medium-high heat. Remove chicken from marinade, reserving marinade. Cook chicken for 3-4 minutes each side or until cooked through.

3 Meanwhile, combine reserved marinade, remaining honey and 1 tablespoon water in a small saucepan over medium-high heat and bring to the boil. Reduce heat to medium and simmer, uncovered, for 3-5 minutes or until mixture has slightly thickened. Strain into a small bowl.

4 Cook noodles following packet instructions or until just tender. Drain. Boil, steam or microwave snow peas, broccolini and asparagus, separately, until just tender. Drain. Divide noodles and vegetables among serving plates. Slice chicken and arrange over noodles. Drizzle with sauce to serve.

NOTE: Soba noodles are thin, pale-brown noodles made with buckwheat flour, which gives them a nutty flavour. Find them in the Asian section of most supermarkets or from Asian grocery stores.

▶ **TIP**

*You can use lean pork steaks instead of chicken. The **ProPoints** values remain the same.*

Spaghetti marinara

 ProPoints VALUES PER SERVE | **SERVES:** 4 | **PREP:** 20 MINS | **COOKING TIME:** 30 MINS

1 tbs olive oil
▲ 1 brown onion, finely chopped
▲ 1 carrot, finely chopped
▲ 1 celery stick, finely chopped
▲ 2 garlic cloves, crushed
3 anchovy fillets, drained, chopped
700ml jar tomato pasta sauce
2 tbs tomato paste
▲ ¼ tsp dried chilli flakes
½ tsp sugar
300g spaghetti pasta
▲ 125g calamari tubes
▲ 125g skinless firm white fish fillet, cut into
2cm pieces (see note)
▲ 250g green prawns, peeled, tails intact
▲ 12 pot-ready mussels (see tip)
▲ 2 tbs chopped fresh flat-leaf parsley leaves

Filling & Healthy Foods are marked with a green triangle.
These foods help fill you up and keep you healthy.

1 Heat oil in a large saucepan over medium heat. Add onion, carrot and celery and cook, stirring, for 6-8 minutes or until softened and lightly golden. Add garlic and anchovy and cooking, stirring, for 3-5 minutes or until anchovy breaks down.
2 Add pasta sauce, tomato paste, chilli and sugar and bring to the boil. Reduce heat and simmer, covered, for 10 minutes or until slightly thickened (add a little water if the sauce is too thick). Season with salt and freshly ground black pepper.
3 Meanwhile, cook pasta in a large saucepan of boiling salted water, following packet instructions, or until just tender. Drain. Cut calamari tubes into 5mm-thick slices.
4 Add calamari, fish, prawns and mussels to sauce. Simmer, covered, for 5 minutes or until seafood is just cooked through and mussels open (discard any that do not open). Serve pasta topped with marinara sauce and sprinkled with parsley.
NOTE: You can use any firm white fish fillet, such as ling, blue-eye trevalla, flathead or snapper. The **ProPoints** values remain the same.
SERVE WITH: 0 **ProPoints** value green salad of mixed lettuce leaves, cucumber, green capsicum and snow pea sprouts, drizzled with lemon juice.

▶ **TIP**
*Pot-ready mussels have been cleaned and the beards removed. Find them at fishmongers or the seafood counter of some supermarkets. To save time, you can use 600g marinara mix instead of buying and preparing individual amounts of seafood. The **ProPoints** values remain the same.*

Vegetarian nachos

 ProPoints VALUES PER SERVE | **SERVES:** 4 | **PREP:** 20 MINS | **COOKING TIME:** 20 MINS

8 x 26g corn tortillas
▲ 2 tomatoes, chopped
▲ ½ red onion, finely chopped
▲ ¼ cup chopped fresh coriander leaves
▲ 1 tbs lime juice
▲ 400g can red kidney beans, rinsed, drained
▲ 310g can corn kernels, drained
200g jar taco sauce
1 cup (120g) Bega So Extra Light grated
   tasty cheese
1 small avocado, mashed
⅓ cup (80g) extra-light sour cream
▲ 1 tbs chopped fresh chives

Filling & Healthy Foods are marked with a green triangle.
These foods help fill you up and keep you healthy.

1 Preheat oven to 200°C or 180°C fan-forced. Lightly spray 2 baking trays with oil. Cut each tortilla into 8 wedges. Arrange on prepared trays and spray lightly with oil. Bake for 8-10 minutes, turning once, until golden and crisp. Cool.

2 Combine tomatoes, onion, coriander and juice in a small bowl. Set salsa aside.

3 Reduce oven to 180°C or 160°C fan-forced. Combine beans, corn and taco sauce in a medium bowl. Arrange tortilla chips around the edge of 4 shallow ovenproof bowls. Top with bean mixture and sprinkle with cheese. Bake for 8-10 minutes or until cheese has melted and is golden.

4 Spoon salsa over nachos. Top with avocado and sour cream and sprinkle with chives. Serve.

▶ TIP
*You can use canned black beans instead of red kidney beans. The **ProPoints** values remain the same.*

THIS MUCH-LOVED MEXICAN MEAL IS A FUN
AND FLAVOURSOME DISH THAT'S IDEAL FOR
FRIDAY-NIGHT COOKING.

Chilli & basil tofu

 ProPoints VALUES PER SERVE | **SERVES:** 4 | **PREP:** 15 MINS | **COOKING TIME:** 15 MINS

2 tbs soy sauce
▲ **2 garlic cloves, crushed**
▲ **2 fresh red birdseye chillies, deseeded, finely chopped**
▲ **300g pkt firm tofu, thinly sliced**
▲ **280g dried soba noodles**
1 tbs sunflower oil
▲ **1 red onion, thinly sliced**
▲ **2 carrots, halved lengthways, thinly sliced**
▲ **1 bunch broccolini, cut into 4cm lengths**
▲ **100g sugar snap peas**
▲ **¼ cup small fresh basil leaves**

Filling & Healthy Foods are marked with a green triangle.
These foods help fill you up and keep you healthy.

1 Combine soy sauce, garlic and chilli in a medium bowl. Add tofu and toss to coat.

2 Cook noodles following packet instructions or until just tender. Drain.

3 Drain tofu, reserving marinade. Heat a wok over high heat. Add half the oil and heat for 10 seconds. Cook tofu, in batches, for 2-3 minutes each side or until golden. Transfer to a plate and cover to keep warm. Heat remaining oil in wok for 10 seconds. Stir-fry onion and carrot for 2 minutes. Add broccolini and stir-fry for 3-4 minutes or until vegetables are tender.

4 Add sugar snap peas and reserved marinade and stir-fry for 1 minute. Add drained noodles and stir-fry until heated through. Divide noodle mixture among serving bowls. Top with tofu and basil. Serve.

► TIP
You can use any dried Asian noodles for this recipe. The **ProPoints** *values remain the same.*

Fragrant baked fish

ProPoints VALUES PER SERVE | **SERVES:** 4 | **PREP:** 15 MINS | **COOKING TIME:** 15 MINS

▲ **2 kaffir lime leaves, torn (see tip)**
▲ **3cm piece fresh ginger, thinly sliced**
▲ **2 garlic cloves, thinly sliced**
▲ **1 fresh red birdseye chilli, deseeded, thinly sliced**
▲ **4 x 150g skinless firm white fish fillets (see note)**
    165ml can light coconut milk
▲ **2 baby bok choy, halved**
▲ **1 carrot, thinly sliced diagonally**
▲ **150g snow peas, halved diagonally**
▲ **Lime wedges**

Filling & Healthy Foods are marked with a green triangle.
These foods help fill you up and keep you healthy.

1 Preheat oven to 200°C or 180°C fan-forced. Lightly spray a 30cm x 20cm baking dish with oil. Arrange kaffir lime leaves, ginger, garlic and chilli over base of prepared dish. Top with fish.

2 Drizzle coconut milk over fish. Cover dish with foil and bake for 12–15 minutes or until fish is just cooked through.

3 Meanwhile, boil, steam or microwave bok choy, carrot and snow peas, separately, until just tender. Drain.

4 Divide vegetables among serving plates. Top with fish and drizzle with pan juices. Serve with lime wedges.

NOTE: You can use any firm white fish fillets, such as ling, blue-eye trevalla, flathead or snapper. The **ProPoints** values remain the same. Thick fillets may take a little longer to cook.

SERVE WITH: Steamed jasmine rice. Add 4 **ProPoints** values per serve for ½ cup (85g).

▶ **TIP**
Kaffir lime leaves have a distinctive hour-glass shape and a strong lime flavour. Find them packed on trays in the fresh produce section of most supermarkets or Asian grocery stores.

Margherita pizza

 ProPoints VALUES PER SERVE | **SERVES:** 4 | **PREP:** 15 MINS | **COOKING TIME:** 1 HOUR 5 MINS, PLUS 10 MINS COOLING

▲ **500g vine-ripened tomatoes, halved**
▲ **1 tsp dried oregano**
  1 tbs olive oil
▲ **1 brown onion, finely chopped**
▲ **2 garlic cloves, crushed**
  2 tbs tomato paste
  2 x 100g wholemeal Lebanese bread rounds
  180g baby bocconcini cheese, halved
▲ **Fresh basil leaves**

Filling & Healthy Foods are marked with a green triangle.
These foods help fill you up and keep you healthy.

1 Preheat oven to 200°C or 180°C fan-forced.
Place tomatoes in a large baking dish. Sprinkle
with oregano and lightly spray with oil. Bake for
40–45 minutes or until softened. Cool for 10 minutes.
Coarsely chop.
2 Heat oil in a small saucepan over medium-high
heat. Add onion and garlic and cook, stirring, for
3–4 minutes or until softened. Add tomato paste,
chopped tomatoes and ½ cup (125ml) water and
bring to the boil. Reduce heat and simmer,
uncovered, for 5 minutes or until thickened.
3 Place bread on 2 baking trays and spread with
tomato mixture. Top with cheese. Bake for
10–12 minutes or until pizza bases are crisp and
cheese has melted. Serve topped with basil.
SERVE WITH: 0 *ProPoints* value mixed leaf salad.

▶**TIP**
*You can use roma tomatoes
instead of vine-ripened tomatoes.
The **ProPoints** values remain
the same.*

Sage & lemon veal with roast potatoes

 ProPoints VALUES PER SERVE | **SERVES:** 4 | **PREP:** 10 MINS | **COOKING TIME:** 30 MINS

▲ **8 baby (chat) potatoes, halved**
  2 tbs finely grated parmesan cheese
▲ **4 x 125g thin lean veal leg steaks**
  1 tbs olive oil
▲ **1 tbs shredded fresh sage leaves**
▲ **¼ cup (60ml) lemon juice**

Filling & Healthy Foods are marked with a green triangle.
These foods help fill you up and keep you healthy.

1 Preheat oven to 200°C or 180°C fan-forced. Lightly spray a baking tray with oil. Place potatoes on a board, cut-side-down, and cut 4 deep parallel cuts into each piece (do not cut all the way through). Place potatoes on prepared tray and lightly spray with oil. Bake for 25-30 minutes or until crisp and tender. Sprinkle with parmesan and bake 5 minutes or until cheese is golden.
2 Meanwhile, pound veal between 2 sheets of plastic wrap until 5mm thick (see tip). Heat oil in a large non-stick frying pan over high heat. Cook veal, in batches, for 1-2 minutes each side or until cooked to your liking. Transfer to a plate and cover to keep warm.
3 Add sage to pan and cook, stirring, for 30 seconds. Add juice and stir, scraping the bottom of the pan, for 1 minute. Place veal on serving plates and drizzle with pan juices. Serve with potatoes.
SERVE WITH: 0 **ProPoints** value steamed baby carrots and baby Brussels sprouts.

▶ **TIP**
Make a few small cuts in the sides of each steak to stop them from curling up during cooking.

SOPHISTICATION MEETS SIMPLE IN THIS ITALIAN-INSPIRED MEAL OF TENDER VEAL AND PARMESAN-TOPPED POTATOES. IT COULD EASILY DOUBLE AS A DINNER-PARTY DISH.

Chermoula braised chicken with barley

 ProPoints VALUES PER SERVE | **SERVES:** 4 | **PREP:** 20 MINS, PLUS 1 HOUR MARINATING | **COOKING TIME:** 1 HOUR
SUITABLE TO FREEZE

▲ ½ cup fresh coriander leaves
▲ ⅓ cup fresh flat-leaf parsley leaves
▲ 2 garlic cloves, crushed
▲ ½ tsp dried red chilli flakes
▲ 2 tsp ground cumin
▲ 2 tbs lemon juice
  500g lean chicken thigh fillets, fat trimmed,
    cut into 4cm pieces
  1 tbs olive oil
▲ 1 red onion, thinly sliced
  3 cups (750ml) chicken stock
▲ ½ cup (100g) pearl barley
  ¼ cup (35g) raisins

Filling & Healthy Foods are marked with a green triangle.
These foods help fill you up and keep you healthy.

1 Place ⅓ cup coriander in a food processor with
parsley, garlic, chilli, cumin and juice. Process until
almost smooth. Add 2 tablespoons hot water and
process to make a smooth paste. Season with salt
and freshly ground black pepper.
2 Combine chicken and half the coriander
mixture in a large glass or ceramic bowl. Cover and
refrigerate for 1 hour.
3 Preheat oven to 180°C or 160°C fan-forced. Heat
half the oil in a large flameproof casserole dish over
high heat. Cook chicken, turning, in batches, for
2-3 minutes or until browned. Transfer to a plate.
4 Heat remaining oil in same dish over medium
heat. Add onion and cook, stirring, for 3-4 minutes
or until softened. Add remaining coriander
mixture and cook, stirring, for 1-2 minutes or until
fragrant. Return chicken to dish with stock, barley
and raisins and bring to the boil. Cover and bake for
45 minutes or until barley is tender. Serve
sprinkled with remaining coriander.
NOTE: Suitable to freeze for up to 3 months.
SERVE WITH: 0 *ProPoints* value steamed green
beans and zucchini.

▶ **TIP**
*You can use brown rice instead
of pearl barley. The **ProPoints**
values remain the same.*

Mushroom quiche

 ProPoints VALUES PER SERVE | **SERVES:** 6 | **PREP:** 25 MINS | **COOKING TIME:** 45 MINS, PLUS COOLING

5 sheets fresh filo pastry (see note)
1 tbs Weight Watchers Canola Spread
▲ **200g button mushrooms, halved**
▲ **200g Swiss brown mushrooms, sliced**
▲ **2 garlic cloves, crushed**
▲ **6 eggs**
▲ **¾ cup (185ml) skim milk**
▲ **2 tbs chopped fresh chives**
¼ cup (20g) finely grated parmesan cheese
▲ **⅓ cup (65g) Weight Watchers Cottage cheese**

Filling & Healthy Foods are marked with a green triangle.
These foods help fill you up and keep you healthy.

1 Preheat oven to 200°C or 180°C fan-forced. Lightly spray a 20cm round (base measurement) springform tin with oil. Place 1 filo sheet on a flat surface and lightly spray with oil. Top with another filo sheet placed at a 45-degree angle and lightly spray with oil. Repeat with remaining filo to make a star-shaped stack. Press stack into prepared tin, tucking in overhanging edges. Place tin on a baking tray.

2 Melt spread in a large non-stick frying pan over medium-high heat. Add mushrooms and cook, stirring, for 4-5 minutes or until golden. Add garlic and cook, stirring, for 30 seconds. Cool slightly.

3 Whisk eggs, milk, chives and parmesan in a large jug. Season with salt and freshly ground black pepper. Spoon cooled mushroom mixture into pastry case. Pour egg mixture over filling and dollop with tablespoons of cottage cheese. Bake for 40-45 minutes or until pastry is golden and filling is set. Remove from oven and set aside for 10 minutes before cutting into wedges.

NOTE: Fresh filo pastry is sold in the chiller cabinets of most supermarkets and is easier to work with than frozen filo.

SERVE WITH: Steamed broccolini drizzled with 2 tablespoons lemon juice, 1 tablespoon olive oil and 1 tablespoon flaked almonds (toasted). Add 2 **ProPoints** values per serve.

Chargrilled vegetable lasagne

 ProPoints VALUES PER SERVE | **SERVES:** 6 | **PREP:** 30 MINS | **COOKING TIME:** 1 HOUR 40 MINS
SUITABLE TO FREEZE

▲ **3 red capsicums**
▲ **1.5kg Kent pumpkin, cut into 2cm cubes**
▲ **1 eggplant, thinly sliced widthways**
▲ **2 zucchini, thinly sliced lengthways**
  **1½ cups (300g) reduced-fat fresh ricotta
  cheese**
▲ **1 garlic clove, crushed**
▲ **¾ cup chopped fresh basil leaves**
▲ **400g can diced tomatoes**
  9 sheets (150g) dried lasagne
  **1 cup (120g) Bega So Extra Light grated
  tasty cheese**
▲ **3 tomatoes, thinly sliced**

Filling & Healthy Foods are marked with a green triangle.
These foods help fill you up and keep you healthy.

1 Preheat oven to 200°C or 180°C fan-forced. Place capsicums in a large baking dish. Bake for 1 hour or until the skin is charred and capsicums are tender. Cover dish and set aside to cool. Peel and discard capsicum skin. Cut capsicums in half and remove seeds.

2 Meanwhile, boil, steam or microwave pumpkin until tender. Mash until smooth and season with salt and freshly ground black pepper.

3 Preheat a barbecue or chargrill over medium-high heat. Lightly spray eggplant and zucchini with oil. Cook, in batches, for 2-3 minutes each side or until tender and slightly charred.

4 Combine ricotta, garlic and basil in a small bowl. Season with salt and freshly ground black pepper.

5 Lightly spray a 2.25L (9-cup) capacity rectangular baking dish with oil. Spread ½ cup (125ml) canned tomato over base of prepared dish. Top with 3 lasagne sheets, breaking to fit. Spread with one-third of the remaining canned tomato and one-third of the pumpkin. Top with capsicum and 3 lasagne sheets. Press down gently. Spread with half the remaining canned tomato and pumpkin. Top with eggplant, overlapping slices slightly. Top with remaining lasagne sheets, canned tomato and pumpkin. Top with zucchini, overlapping slices slightly. Spread ricotta mixture over zucchini. Sprinkle with one-third of the cheese and top with sliced tomato, overlapping slices slightly. Sprinkle with remaining cheese.

6 Bake for 40 minutes or until top is golden and pasta is tender. Set aside for 5 minutes before serving.

SERVE WITH: O **ProPoints** value salad of rocket leaves drizzled with balsamic vinegar.

Miso-marinated beef with ginger carrot mash

 ProPoints VALUES PER SERVE | **SERVES:** 4 | **PREP:** 15 MINS, PLUS 30 MINS MARINATING
COOKING TIME: 20 MINS

1 tbs miso paste (see note)
2 tbs mirin (Japanese rice wine)
2 tbs reduced-salt soy sauce
▲ 1 garlic clove, crushed
4 x 125g lean beef fillet steaks, fat trimmed
▲ 500g carrots, chopped
▲ 300g sweet potato (kumara), chopped
2 tsp sesame oil
▲ 1 tsp finely grated fresh ginger
▲ 4 green shallots, thinly sliced

Filling & Healthy Foods are marked with a green triangle.
These foods help fill you up and keep you healthy.

1 Combine miso, mirin, soy sauce and garlic in a shallow glass or ceramic dish. Add steaks and turn to coat. Cover and refrigerate for 30 minutes.

2 Boil, steam or microwave carrot and sweet potato until tender. Drain.

3 Meanwhile, preheat a chargrill or barbecue over high heat. Cook steaks for 2–3 minutes each side or until cooked to your liking. Transfer to a plate. Cover steaks with foil and set aside to rest for 5 minutes.

4 Heat oil in a medium saucepan over medium heat. Cook ginger and shallots, stirring, for 1 minute or until fragrant. Add carrots and sweet potato and stir to combine. Remove from heat. Using a fork, roughly mash carrot mixture. Season with salt and freshly ground black pepper. Drizzle steaks with any pan juices and serve with mash.

NOTE: Popular in Japanese soups and stews, miso is a salty paste made from fermented soy beans. Find it in the Asian section of most supermarkets or from Asian grocery stores.

A FEW CLASSIC JAPANESE INGREDIENTS CAN TRANSFORM A BASIC STEAK AND MASH MEAL INTO AN ASIAN FLAVOUR SENSATION.

Easy pork & prawn larb

 ProPoints VALUES PER SERVE | **SERVES:** 4 | **PREP:** 15 MINS | **COOKING TIME:** 15 MINS

1 tbs canola oil

▲ 2 garlic cloves, crushed

▲ 2 tsp finely chopped fresh lemongrass

▲ 2 tsp finely grated fresh ginger

500g lean pork mince

▲ 100g peeled green prawns, chopped

▲ 150g fresh pineapple, chopped

▲ 3 green shallots, thinly sliced, plus 1 extra
finely shredded to garnish

2 tbs brown sugar

2 tbs fish sauce

½ cup (125ml) chicken stock

▲ ½ cup loosely packed fresh Thai basil leaves
(see note)

▲ 3 cups (90g) coarsely shredded iceberg
lettuce

Filling & Healthy Foods are marked with a green triangle.
These foods help fill you up and keep you healthy.

1 Heat a wok over medium-high heat. Add oil and heat for 10 seconds. Stir-fry garlic, lemongrass and ginger for 30 seconds. Add pork and prawns and stir-fry, breaking up any lumps, for 5 minutes or until pork has browned and prawns have just changed colour.

2 Add pineapple, sliced shallots, brown sugar, fish sauce and stock and bring to the boil. Reduce heat and simmer for 6-8 minutes or until liquid has evaporated.

3 Add basil and toss to combine. Serve larb with shredded shallots and lettuce.

NOTE: Thai basil has purplish stems and small leaves with a strong aniseed taste. Find it in bunches in the fresh produce section of most supermarkets or from Asian grocery stores. If unavailable use fresh coriander leaves.

SERVE WITH: Steamed jasmine rice. Add 4 **ProPoints** values per serve for ½ cup (85g).

▶ **TIP**

You can use chicken mince instead of pork. The **ProPoints** values remain the same.

EVERY GREEK COOK HAS THEIR OWN
SPECIAL SPIN ON THIS TRADITIONAL
EGGPLANT DISH BUT WE THINK OUR
VERSION IS QUITE DELISH!

Moussaka rolls

ProPoints VALUES PER SERVE | **SERVES:** 4 | **PREP:** 30 MINS | **COOKING TIME:** 45 MINS
SUITABLE TO FREEZE

▲ **2 medium eggplants**
  1 tbs olive oil
▲ **1 brown onion, finely chopped**
▲ **2 garlic cloves, crushed**
  400g lean lamb mince
▲ **½ tsp ground cinnamon**
▲ **½ tsp ground allspice**
  1 tbs tomato paste
▲ **400g can diced tomatoes**
▲ **2 tbs finely chopped fresh oregano leaves**
  1½ cups (375ml) tomato pasta sauce
  ⅓ cup (40g) Bega So Extra Light grated tasty cheese

Filling & Healthy Foods are marked with a green triangle.
These foods help fill you up and keep you healthy.

1 Preheat oven to 200°C or 180°C fan-forced. Lightly spray a 2L (8-cup) capacity ovenproof dish with oil. Trim 1cm from each end of eggplants. Slice each eggplant lengthways into 6 thin slices. Heat a chargrill or barbecue over medium-high heat. Lightly spray both sides of eggplant slices with oil. Cook eggplant, in batches, for 2-3 minutes each side or until lightly charred.

2 Heat oil in a large non-stick frying pan over medium heat. Cook half the onion, stirring, for 3-4 minutes or until softened. Add half the garlic and cook, stirring, for 1 minute. Add lamb, cinnamon and allspice and cook, breaking up any lumps, for 5 minutes or until browned. Add paste and tomatoes and bring to the boil. Reduce heat and simmer, uncovered, for 10-15 minutes or until thickened. Remove from heat and stir in half the oregano.

3 Meanwhile, lightly spray a medium saucepan with oil and heat over medium heat. Cook remaining onion, stirring, for 3-4 minutes or until softened. Add remaining garlic and cook, stirring, for 1 minute. Add pasta sauce and remaining oregano and bring to the boil. Reduce heat and simmer for 5 minutes or until sauce has slightly thickened. Spread one-third of sauce over base of prepared dish.

4 Place eggplant slices on a flat surface. Divide lamb mixture across centre of eggplant slices. Roll eggplant to enclose filling and place, seam-side down, in prepared dish. Pour remaining pasta sauce mixture over moussaka rolls. Sprinkle with cheese and bake for 10-15 minutes or until cheese has melted and is golden. Serve.

NOTE: Lamb mixture suitable to freeze for up to 3 months.

SERVE WITH: Salad of baby spinach leaves, baby roma tomatoes (halved), Lebanese cucumber (chopped) and 1 avocado (chopped), drizzled with fat-free French dressing. Add 2 **ProPoints** values per serve for avocado.

Prosciutto-wrapped pork on lentils

 ProPoints VALUES PER SERVE | **SERVES:** 4 | **PREP:** 15 MINS | **COOKING TIME:** 15 MINS

1 tbs olive oil
▲ **1 red onion, finely chopped**
▲ **2 celery sticks, finely chopped**
▲ **1 carrot, finely chopped**
▲ **2 garlic cloves, crushed**
▲ **1 tsp fresh thyme leaves, plus extra sprigs**
     to garnish
▲ **2 x 400g cans brown lentils, rinsed, drained**
   ½ cup (125ml) chicken stock
   2 tsp balsamic vinegar
   4 (60g) thin slices prosciutto, fat trimmed
▲ **4 x 125g lean pork loin steaks, fat trimmed**

Filling & Healthy Foods are marked with a green triangle.
These foods help fill you up and keep you healthy.

1 Heat oil in a medium saucepan over medium heat. Add onion, celery and carrot and cook, stirring, for 5 minutes or until softened. Add garlic and thyme and cook for 1 minute. Add lentils and stock and bring to the boil. Reduce heat and simmer, uncovered, for 2-3 minutes or until liquid has evaporated by half. Stir in vinegar. Season with salt and freshly ground black pepper. Cover to keep warm.

2 Meanwhile, wrap a piece of prosciutto around the centre of each pork steak. Lightly spray a large non-stick frying pan with oil and heat over medium-high heat. Cook pork for 3-4 minutes each side or until cooked to your liking. Transfer to a plate. Cover pork with foil and set aside to rest for 5 minutes. Serve pork with lentil mixture and a thyme sprig.

SERVE WITH: 0 **ProPoints** value steamed cavalo nero (also called Tuscan cabbage or kale).

► **TIP**
*You can use lean chicken breast fillets instead of pork (increase cooking time by 2–3 minutes). The **ProPoints** values remain the same.*

10 Simple dinner ideas

1 Coriander salmon with sweet chilli sauce

 ProPoints VALUES PER SERVE | **SERVES:** 1

Press ▲ **1 tsp coriander seeds** (crushed) onto a **120g salmon fillet**. Heat **1 tsp canola oil** in a non-stick frying pan over medium heat. Cook salmon until cooked to your liking. Meanwhile, steam ▲ **5 snow peas**, ▲ **5 green beans** and ▲ **1 baby bok choy** (halved) until just tender. Drizzle salmon with **1 tbs sweet chilli sauce** and serve with vegies, ▲ **½ cup cooked brown rice** and a ▲ **lime wedge**.

2 Pan-fried pork with pears

 ProPoints VALUES PER SERVE | **SERVES:** 1

Heat **1 tsp sunflower oil** in a non-stick frying pan over medium heat. Cook a ▲ **150g lean pork butterfly steak** (fat trimmed) until cooked to your liking. Transfer to a plate and cover to keep warm. Add ▲ **1 pear** (sliced) to same pan and cook until golden. Transfer to plate with pork. Add ▲ **1 cup shredded silverbeet** to same pan and cook until wilted. Meanwhile, steam ▲ **¼ corn cob**, ▲ **3 broccolini stems** and ▲ **½ cup chopped sweet potato (kumara)** until just tender. Mash sweet potato and top with pork and pears. Serve with vegetables.

3 Roast chicken & mustard yoghurt sauce

 ProPoints VALUES PER SERVE | **SERVES:** 1

Combine ▲ **¼ cup low-fat natural yoghurt**, **1 tsp wholegrain mustard** and ▲ **1 tsp lemon juice** in a small bowl. Steam ▲ **2 baby (chat) potatoes**, ▲ **¼ cup green peas**, ▲ **½ cup cauliflower florets** and ▲ **½ cup broccoli florets** until just tender. Serve vegetables with ▲ **100g skinless lean roast chicken** drizzled with yoghurt sauce.

4 Moroccan lamb with vegetable couscous

 ProPoints VALUES PER SERVE | **SERVES:** 1

Preheat grill on medium. Rub **1 tsp Moroccan seasoning** over a **60g lean lamb chump chop** (fat trimmed). Grill until cooked to your liking. Meanwhile, combine **½ cup cooked couscous**, ▲ **1 cup baby rocket leaves**, **10 pistachio kernels**, **3 semi-dried tomatoes** (not in oil), ▲ **½ cup chopped red capsicum**, ▲ **½ Lebanese cucumber** (chopped), ▲ **1 tbs fresh coriander leaves**, juice of ▲ **½ lemon** and **1 tsp olive oil** in a bowl. Slice lamb and serve over couscous.

5 Teriyaki tofu skewers

 ProPoints VALUES PER SERVE | **SERVES:** 1

Preheat grill on high. Combine ▲ **150g firm tofu** (cut into 2cm pieces) and **¼ cup teriyaki marinade** in a bowl. Thread tofu onto 2 skewers and grill until heated. Meanwhile, steam ▲ **2 Chinese broccoli (gai lan) stems** (chopped), ▲ **4 fresh baby corn** and ▲ **½ cup sugar snap peas** until just tender. Drizzle vegetables with **½ tsp sesame oil** and serve with skewers and ▲ **½ cup cooked brown rice**.

6 Chicken & shiitake noodle stir-fry

 ProPoints VALUES PER SERVE | **SERVES:** 1

Heat a wok over high heat. Add **1 tsp sunflower oil** and heat for 30 seconds. Stir-fry ▲ **1 garlic clove** (chopped), ▲ **1 tsp grated fresh ginger**, ▲ **½ onion** (chopped) and ▲ **100g lean chicken breast strips** until lightly browned. Add ▲ **½ red capsicum** (sliced), ▲ **4 shiitake mushrooms** (sliced), **1 cup cooked rice noodles** and **1 tbs soy sauce** and stir-fry for 2–3 minutes. Serve topped with ▲ **1 cup bean sprouts** and ▲ **1 green shallot** (chopped).

7 Warm chickpea, tomato & spinach salad

 8 ProPoints VALUES PER SERVE | **SERVES:** 1

Heat **1 tsp olive oil** in a non-stick frying pan over medium heat. Add ▲ **1 garlic clove** (chopped), ▲ **½ tsp smoked paprika**, ▲ **1 tomato** (diced), **½ cup cooked spiral pasta** and ▲ **½ cup drained canned chickpeas** and cook, stirring, until warmed through. Remove from heat and add ▲ **¼ red onion** (sliced), juice of ▲ **½ lemon**, ▲ **1 tbs chopped fresh mint** and ▲ **1 cup baby spinach leaves**. Toss to combine and serve sprinkled with **30g reduced-fat feta cheese** (crumbled).

---

8 Yellow snapper with coriander rice & vegies

 7 ProPoints VALUES PER SERVE | **SERVES:** 1

Rub a ▲ **165g snapper fillet** with ▲ **1 tsp ground turmeric**. Heat **1 tsp sunflower oil** in a non-stick frying pan over high heat. Cook snapper until cooked to your liking. Meanwhile, steam ▲ **1 cup baby spinach leaves**, ▲ **2 yellow baby squash** and ▲ **3 baby carrots** until just tender. Combine **½ cup cooked basmati rice** and ▲ **1 tbs chopped fresh coriander**. Serve snapper with rice and vegies.

---

9 Veal cutlet with lemon thyme mash & cabbage

 7 ProPoints VALUES PER SERVE | **SERVES:** 1

Preheat grill on high. Grill a ▲ **130g lean veal cutlet** (fat trimmed) until cooked to your liking. Mash ▲ **½ cup cooked chopped potato** with **1 tsp olive oil**, ▲ **1 tsp lemon juice** and ▲ **1 tsp fresh lemon thyme**. Meanwhile, steam ▲ **1 cup shredded green cabbage** and ▲ **5 green beans** until just tender. Serve vegies with veal and mash.

10 Balsamic steak with tomato, asparagus & barley salad

 10 ProPoints VALUES PER SERVE | **SERVES:** 1

Combine **1 tbs balsamic vinegar** and ▲ **1 garlic clove** (crushed) in a glass or ceramic dish. Add a ▲ **220g lean beef sirloin steak** (fat trimmed) and turn to coat. Cover and refrigerate for 30 minutes. Preheat a chargrill or barbecue over medium heat. Cook steak until cooked to your liking. Meanwhile, cook ▲ **1 zucchini** (thinly sliced), ▲ **6 cherry tomatoes** and ▲ **4 asparagus spears**, turning, until tender. Toss vegetables with ▲ **½ cup cooked pearl barley**, ▲ **1 tbs chopped fresh flat-leaf parsley**, **1 tsp flaxseed oil** and juice of ▲ **½ lemon**. Slice steak and serve with salad.

SUGAR, SPICE AND
ALL THINGS NICE – THAT'S
EXACTLY WHAT THESE
MOUTH-WATERING
DESSERTS ARE MADE OF!

Sweet & dreamy
DESSERTS

Pavlova with berries & raspberry sauce

 ProPoints VALUES PER SERVE | **SERVES:** 8 | **PREP:** 20 MINS | **COOKING TIME:** 1 HOUR, PLUS COOLING

▲ **6 egg whites**
1 cup (220g) caster sugar
1 tsp vanilla essence
1 tsp white vinegar
3 tsp cornflour
2 x 150g tubs 98% fat-free strawberry fromage frais
▲ **100g Nestlé Soleil Vanilla Flavoured Yoghurt**
▲ **125g fresh raspberries**
▲ **250g fresh strawberries, halved (quartered if large)**
▲ **125g fresh blueberries**
120ml pkt Weight Watchers Raspberry Dessert Sauce (see note)

Filling & Healthy Foods are marked with a green triangle. These foods help fill you up and keep you healthy.

1 Preheat oven to 160°C or 140°C fan-forced. Draw a 23cm circle on a sheet of baking paper and place on a baking tray.

2 Using electric beaters, beat egg whites in a clean, dry bowl until soft peaks form. Gradually add sugar, 1 tablespoon at a time, beating well after each addition until sugar has dissolved. Fold in vanilla, vinegar and cornflour (see tip).

3 Spoon mixture onto prepared circle and make a slight indentation in the centre. Bake for 1 hour or until pavlova is firm. Turn off oven. Leave pavlova in oven, door slightly ajar, until cool.

4 Combine fromage frais and yoghurt in a medium bowl. Spoon mixture onto pavlova and top with raspberries, strawberries and blueberries. Drizzle pavlova with half the dessert sauce. Serve with remaining sauce.

NOTE: Weight Watchers Raspberry Dessert Sauce is available from Weight Watchers meetings or from our online shop (weightwatchers.com.au or weightwatchers.co.nz). Alternatively, you can use a raspberry dessert sauce from the gourmet section of the supermarket. The **ProPoints** values remain the same.

▶**TIP**
Use a metal spoon to fold the ingredients through the beaten egg whites as it will 'cut' through the mixture without deflating too many air bubbles.

Passionfruit & coconut crème brûlées

 ProPoints VALUES PER SERVE | **SERVES:** 4 | **PREP:** 20 MINS | **COOKING TIME:** 35 MINS, PLUS COOLING & OVERNIGHT SETTING

▲ **1 egg**
▲ **2 egg yolks**
2 tbs caster sugar
▲ **¼ cup (60ml) fresh passionfruit pulp (see tip)**
375ml can coconut-flavoured evaporated milk
1 tbs grated palm sugar

Filling & Healthy Foods are marked with a green triangle.
These foods help fill you up and keep you healthy.

1 Preheat oven to 180°C or 160°C fan-forced. Place four ¾-cup (185ml) capacity ramekins in a large baking dish.
2 Whisk egg, egg yolks, caster sugar and passionfruit in a medium bowl until smooth. Place evaporated milk in a small saucepan over medium heat and bring to the boil. Gradually whisk hot milk into egg mixture. Pour custard into a heatproof jug.
3 Divide custard among ramekins. Pour enough boiling water into baking dish to come halfway up sides of ramekins. Bake for 25-30 minutes or until firm to touch. Remove ramekins from baking dish and cool for 20 minutes. Refrigerate overnight.
4 Preheat grill on high. Place custards in shallow flameproof dish filled with ice cubes (see note). Sprinkle each custard with 1 teaspoon palm sugar. Using your finger, gently smooth sugar over surface of each custard. Grill until tops of crème brûlées caramelise. Serve.
NOTE: Surrounding the ramekins with ice during grilling helps to keep the brûlées cold while the sugar melts.

▶ **TIP**
You will need 3 medium fresh passionfruit for this recipe.

BRING A TASTE OF THE TROPICS TO YOUR TABLE WITH THIS DELECTABLE DESSERT. EACH SPOONFUL OF CREAMY COCONUT-FLAVOURED CUSTARD IS LIKE AN ISLAND HOLIDAY.

Apricot crumble tarts

ProPoints VALUES PER SERVE | **SERVES:** 4 | **PREP:** 25 MINS | **COOKING TIME:** 35 MINS, PLUS COOLING

**1 sheet frozen reduced-fat shortcrust pastry,
just thawed**
▲ **400g can Weight Watchers Halved Apricots**
▲ **1 vanilla bean, halved**
1 tbs caster sugar
2 tbs plain flour
2 tsp desiccated coconut
15g Weight Watchers Canola Spread

Filling & Healthy Foods are marked with a green triangle.
These foods help fill you up and keep you healthy.

1 Preheat oven to 200°C or 180°C fan-forced.
Lightly spray four ⅓-cup (80ml) capacity muffin tin
holes with oil.

2 Using a 9.5cm fluted cutter, cut 4 rounds from
pastry. Line prepared muffin holes with pastry.
Line pastry cases with baking paper and fill with
pastry weights, dried beans or rice. Bake for
15 minutes. Remove paper and weights.

3 Meanwhile, drain apricots, reserving syrup.
Scrape seeds from vanilla bean (see tip), reserving
pod. Combine apricots, half the sugar, vanilla
seeds and pod and 2 tablespoons reserved syrup
in a small saucepan over medium heat and bring
to the boil. Reduce heat and simmer, uncovered,
for 5 minutes or until thickened. Transfer to a bowl.
Discard vanilla pod. Cool.

4 Combine flour, remaining sugar and coconut
in a bowl. Using fingertips, rub in spread until
mixture resembles coarse breadcrumbs. Spoon
apricot mixture into pastry cases. Top with crumble
mixture and bake for 20 minutes or until lightly
browned. Carefully remove tarts from tin. Serve
warm or cold.

NOTE: You can store these tarts in an airtight
container in the fridge for up to 3 days.

▶ TIP

*Use a small sharp knife to cut
lengthways down the vanilla bean.
Then use the tip of the knife to
scrape the tiny black seeds out
of the pod.*

Easy cappuccino parfaits

 ProPoints VALUES PER SERVE | **SERVES:** 4 | **PREP:** 15 MINS, PLUS 3 HOURS SETTING

3 tsp instant coffee granules
▲ **300g low-fat smooth ricotta cheese**
▲ **¾ cup (200g) no-fat Greek-style natural
   yoghurt**
   ¼ cup (40g) icing sugar
   **6 (60g) Weight Watchers Chocolate Chip
   Cookies, crumbled**

Filling & Healthy Foods are marked with a green triangle.
These foods help fill you up and keep you healthy.

1 Combine coffee and 3 tsp boiling water in a small
bowl until coffee has dissolved. Cool.
2 Place ricotta, yoghurt, icing sugar and coffee
mixture in a food processor. Process until smooth.
3 Divide half the ricotta mixture among four
⅔-cup (160ml) capacity serving glasses. Sprinkle
two-thirds of cookie pieces evenly over ricotta
mixture. Top with remaining ricotta mixture and
remaining cookie pieces. Cover and refrigerate for
3 hours or until set. Serve.

▶ **TIP**

*To make a mocha parfait, add
1 tbs cocoa powder to the coffee
mixture. The recipe will then have
6 ProPoints values per serve.*

THIS TRADITIONAL ENGLISH PUDDING
IS AS PRETTY AS IT IS SIMPLE. WHEN THE
BERRY SYRUP SOAKS INTO THE BREAD IT
CREATES A STUNNING PURPLE HUE.

Summer pudding

 7 | **ProPoints** VALUES PER SERVE | **SERVES:** 4 | **PREP:** 20 MINS | **COOKING TIME:** 5 MINS, PLUS OVERNIGHT REFRIGERATION

▲ **250g fresh or frozen raspberries,**
▲ **250g fresh or frozen blueberries**
▲ **1 vanilla bean (see tip)**
▲ **250g fresh strawberries**
  ½ cup (110g) caster sugar
  8 x 32g slices wholemeal bread,
    crusts removed

Filling & Healthy Foods are marked with a green triangle.
These foods help fill you up and keep you healthy.

1 Reserve 50g each of the raspberries and blueberries. Scrape seeds from vanilla bean and discard pod (see tip). Place strawberries, sugar, vanilla seeds, ¼ cup (60ml) water and remaining raspberries and blueberries in a medium saucepan over medium heat. Cook, stirring, for 3-4 minutes or until sugar has dissolved. Strain into a medium bowl, reserving the liquid.

2 Lightly spray a 1L (4-cup) capacity pudding basin with oil. Cut each bread slice in half. Working with 1 piece at a time, dip 12 bread halves into reserved berry liquid for 10 seconds and line the base and sides of the pudding bowl. Spoon berry mixture into centre of bread casing. Dip remaining 4 bread halves into remaining berry liquid and cover top of the berries. Tightly wrap pudding with plastic wrap and refrigerate overnight.

3 Turn pudding out onto a serving plate and serve with reserved berries.

SERVE WITH: Weight Watchers Creamy Vanilla Ice Cream. Add 1 **ProPoints** value per serve for half a 145ml tub.

▶ **TIP**

Use a small sharp knife to cut lengthways down the vanilla bean. Then use the tip of the knife to scrape the tiny black seeds out of the pod. You can place the pod in a container of caster sugar to add extra flavour to baking.

Chocolate puddings with chocolate sauce

 ProPoints VALUES PER SERVE | **SERVES:** 4 | **PREP:** 15 MINS | **COOKING TIME:** 15 MINS

¼ cup (60g) Weight Watchers Canola Spread
⅓ cup (75g) firmly packed brown sugar
▲ 1 egg, lightly beaten
▲ ¼ cup (60ml) skim milk
1 tsp vanilla extract
¾ cup (110g) self-raising flour
¼ cup (25g) cocoa powder, plus 1 tbs for sauce
½ cup (125ml) skim condensed milk
▲ 250g fresh strawberries, sliced

Filling & Healthy Foods are marked with a green triangle.
These foods help fill you up and keep you healthy.

1 Preheat oven to 180°C or 160°C fan-forced. Lightly spray four ¾-cup (185ml) capacity ovenproof dishes with oil and line bases with baking paper.
2 Using electric beaters, beat spread and brown sugar in a small bowl for 3-4 minutes or until pale and creamy. Beat in egg, then skim milk and vanilla. Gently fold in sifted flour and ¼ cup (25g) cocoa until just combined.
3 Spoon mixture into prepared dishes. Bake for 15-20 minutes or until just firm to the touch.
4 Meanwhile, combine condensed milk and 1 tablespoon cocoa in a small saucepan over low heat. Stir until heated through. Turn puddings out onto serving plates. Spoon sauce over puddings and serve with strawberries.

Baked apples with pecans & fig

 ProPoints VALUES PER SERVE | **SERVES:** 4 | **PREP:** 15 MINS | **COOKING TIME:** 30 MINS

40g Weight Watchers Canola Spread
2 tbs brown sugar
1 tbs sultanas
2 dried figs, finely chopped
1 tbs pecans, finely chopped
▲ **4 medium red apples**
▲ **½ cup (140g) Nestlé Soleil Vanilla Flavoured Yoghurt**

Filling & Healthy Foods are marked with a green triangle.
These foods help fill you up and keep you healthy.

1 Preheat oven to 180°C or 160°C fan-forced.
Combine spread, sugar, sultanas, figs and pecans
in a small bowl.

2 Using a small, sharp knife or apple corer, core the
unpeeled apples without cutting all the way
through to the base. The holes should be about
4cm in diameter and finish 2cm from the base.
Use same knife to score a shallow cut around the
centre of each apple (see note). Stand apples
upright in a small ovenproof dish.

3 Spoon pecan mixture into cavity of each apple.
Bake for 30-35 minutes or until apples are
tender. Drizzle with pan juices and serve with
yoghurt.

NOTE: Scoring the apple stops the skin from
splitting as it bakes.

▶ **TIP**
*You can use dried dates and
walnuts instead of dried figs
and pecans. The **ProPoints**
values remain the same.*

Choc-orange baklava stacks

 ProPoints VALUES PER SERVE | **SERVES:** 4 | **PREP:** 30 MINS | **COOKING TIME:** 15 MINS

⅓ cup (50g) unsalted pistachio kernels
2 sheets fresh filo pastry
▲ ½ tsp ground cinnamon
⅓ cup (80ml) orange juice
1 tbs honey
4 x 62g tubs Nestlé® Soleil™ Chocolate Mousse
▲ 2 oranges, segmented (see tip)
▲ 200g fresh strawberries, thinly sliced

Filling & Healthy Foods are marked with a green triangle.
These foods help fill you up and keep you healthy.

1 Preheat oven to 200°C or 180°C fan-forced. Spread pistachios on a baking tray and bake for 2-3 minutes or until toasted. Finely chop.

2 Line a baking tray with baking paper. Place 1 filo sheet on a flat surface and lightly spray with oil. Top with remaining filo sheet and lightly spray with oil. Cut pastry stack in half lengthways, then cut each piece crossways into 8 rectangles to make 16 rectangles.

3 Combine pistachios and cinnamon in a small bowl. Reserve 1 teaspoon of mixture. Place 4 filo rectangles on prepared tray. Sprinkle each with 1 teaspoon of pistachio mixture. Repeat layering with remaining filo and pistachio mixture to make 4 stacks. Bake for 10-12 minutes or until golden. Cool.

4 Meanwhile, combine juice and honey in a small saucepan over medium heat and bring to the boil. Reduce heat and simmer for 10 minutes or until syrup has thickened.

5 Place filo stacks onto serving plates. Carefully lift off top layer and spoon **Nestlé® Soleil™ Chocolate Mousse** over base. Top with orange, strawberries and pastry tops. Drizzle with syrup and sprinkle with reserved pistachio mixture. Serve.

▶TIP

To segment an orange, use a sharp knife to cut off the rind and pith. Holding the orange over a bowl to catch any juice, carefully cut segments from between the membranes.

Cherry yoghurt iceblocks

 ProPoints VALUE PER ICEBLOCK | **MAKES:** 10 | **PREP:** 10 MINS, PLUS 4 HOURS FREEZING

▲ **100g frozen pitted cherries**
▲ **2 cups (560g) Nestlé® Soleil™ Vanilla
    Flavoured Yoghurt**
▲ **1 egg white**
    1 tbs caster sugar

Filling & Healthy Foods are marked with a green triangle.
These foods help fill you up and keep you healthy.

1 Place cherries and **Nestlé® Soleil™ Vanilla
Flavoured Yoghurt** in a blender or food processor.
Blend until smooth.
2 Using electric beaters, beat egg white in a small,
clean, dry bowl until soft peaks form. Add sugar
and beat until thick and glossy. Fold meringue
through cherry mixture.
3 Spoon mixture into ten ¼-cup (60ml) capacity
iceblock moulds. Insert sticks and freeze for
4 hours or until hard.
4 Dip moulds in hot water for 5-10 seconds and
gently pull out iceblocks. Serve.

Blueberry banana creams

 ProPoints VALUE PER SERVE | **SERVES:** 4 | **PREP:** 10 MINS, PLUS 2 HOURS SETTING

2 tsp gelatine powder
▲ **2 bananas, chopped**
▲ **1 cup (280g) Nestlé® Soleil™ Vanilla Flavoured Yoghurt**
▲ **½ tsp finely grated lemon rind**
▲ **1 tbs lemon juice**
▲ **100g fresh or thawed frozen blueberries**

Filling & Healthy Foods are marked with a green triangle. These foods help fill you up and keep you healthy.

1 Place 2 tablespoons boiling water in a small jug and sprinkle with gelatine. Whisk with a fork until gelatine has dissolved. Place bananas, **Nestlé® Soleil™ Vanilla Flavoured Yoghurt**, rind, juice and gelatine mixture in a food processor. Process for 1 minute or until smooth.
2 Spoon mixture into four ½-cup (125ml) capacity serving glasses. Refrigerate for 2 hours or until set. Top with blueberries to serve.

10 Simple dessert ideas

1 Banana ice-cream

 ProPoints VALUE PER SERVE | **SERVES:** 1

Place ▲ **1 banana** (cut into small pieces) in a freezerproof bowl and freeze for 1-2 hours or until firm. Process in a small food processor or blender until smooth and creamy. Serve.

2 Melon salad with passionfruit yoghurt

 ProPoints VALUES PER SERVE | **SERVES:** 1

Combine ▲ **¼ cup chopped watermelon**, ▲ **¼ cup chopped rockmelon** and ▲ **¼ cup chopped honeydew melon** in a bowl. Top with ▲ **150g tub Nestlé Soleil Passionfruit Yoghurt** and pulp of ▲ **1 passionfruit**. Serve.

3 Pineapple, macadamia & coconut yoghurt parfait

 ProPoints VALUES PER SERVE | **SERVES:** 1

Place **1 tbs shredded coconut** in a small non-stick frying pan over medium heat. Cook, stirring, until golden. Combine half the coconut with ▲ **150g tub Nestlé Soleil Vanilla Flavoured Yoghurt** in a small bowl. Layer yoghurt mixture in a tall glass with ▲ **1 cup chopped fresh pineapple** and **10g macadamia nuts** (chopped). Sprinkle with remaining coconut. Serve.

4 Grilled maple peach with hazelnuts

 ProPoints VALUES PER SERVE | **SERVES:** 1

Preheat grill on high. Grill ▲ **1 peach** (halved, stone removed) until softened. Drizzle with **1 tsp maple syrup** and sprinkle with **10 roasted hazelnuts** (chopped). Serve.

5 Cherry choc meringue

 ProPoints VALUES PER SERVE | **SERVES:** 1

Spoon **2 tbs 99% fat-free vanilla fromage frais** into a **25g meringue nest**. Top with ▲ **½ cup pitted cherries**. Process another ▲ **½ cup pitted cherries** in a small food processor or blender until smooth. Serve meringue drizzled with cherry puree and sprinkled with **1 square dark chocolate** (grated).

6 Berries with honey & spice ricotta

 ProPoints VALUES PER SERVE | **SERVES:** 1

Combine ▲ **½ cup low-fat smooth ricotta cheese**, **1 tsp honey** and a **pinch mixed spice** in a small bowl. Serve with ▲ **1 cup fresh or thawed frozen mixed berries**.

7 Baked apple with dates & walnuts

 ProPoints VALUES PER SERVE | **SERVES:** 1

Preheat oven to 200°C or 180°C fan-forced. Place **1 red apple** (unpeeled, cored, scored around the middle) in a baking dish. Stuff with **2 fresh dates** (halved, stone removed) and **4 walnut pieces**. Top with **1 tsp Weight Watchers Canola Spread** and sprinkle with **1 tsp brown sugar** and a ▲ **pinch ground cinnamon**. Bake for 30 minutes or until tender. Serve with ▲ **3 tbs Nestlé Soleil Vanilla Flavoured Yoghurt**.

---

8 Watermelon, strawberries & rosewater ice-cream

 ProPoints VALUES PER SERVE | **SERVES:** 1

Combine ▲ **1 cup chopped watermelon** and ▲ **½ cup chopped fresh strawberries** in a serving bowl. Add **2 drops rosewater** to a **145ml tub Weight Watchers Creamy Vanilla Ice Cream** and stir to combine. Scoop ice-cream onto fruit and sprinkle with **10 unsalted pistachio kernels** (chopped). Serve.

---

9 Ginger chocolate mousse

 ProPoints VALUES PER SERVE | **SERVES:** 1

Combine **1 ginger biscuit** (crumbled), **62g tub Nestlé Soleil Dark Chocolate Mousse** and **1 piece crystallised ginger** (chopped) in a small bowl. Serve.

10 Spiced poached pear with nutmeg custard

ProPoints VALUES PER SERVE | **SERVES:** 1

Place ▲ **1 pear** (halved), **1 cup water**, **1 tsp sugar**, ▲ **½ cinnamon stick** and ▲ **½ split vanilla bean** in a small saucepan and bring to the boil. Reduce heat and simmer until pear is tender. Discard cinnamon and vanilla bean. Combine **½ cup reduced-fat custard** with a ▲ **pinch ground nutmeg** in a small saucepan over low heat until warmed through. Drizzle pear with a little poaching liquid and serve with custard.

WHEN FRIENDS
POP AROUND FOR
MORNING OR
AFTERNOON TEA,
SHOW OFF YOUR NEW
CULINARY SKILLS WITH
THESE SWEET AND
SAVOURY TREATS.

Tea-time
TREATS

Carrot & banana muffins

 ProPoints VALUES PER MUFFIN | **MAKES:** 12 | **PREP:** 15 MINS | **COOKING TIME:** 20 MINS | SUITABLE TO FREEZE

1½ cups (225g) self-raising flour
▲ **1 tsp ground cinnamon**
▲ **2 small ripe bananas, mashed**
¾ cup (185ml) buttermilk
▲ **1 egg**
¼ cup (60ml) honey
1 tsp vanilla extract
2 tbs canola oil
▲ **1 cup (140g) grated carrot (see tip)**
2 tsp icing sugar

Filling & Healthy Foods are marked with a green triangle.
These foods help fill you up and keep you healthy.

1 Preheat oven to 180°C or 160°C fan forced. Line a 12-hole (⅓-cup/80ml capacity) muffin tin with paper cases.
2 Sift flour and cinnamon into a large mixing bowl. Mix banana, buttermilk, egg, honey, vanilla and oil in a separate bowl until combined. Add banana mixture to flour mixture and stir until just combined (do not over-mix). Gently fold in carrot.
3 Spoon mixture into paper cases. Bake for 18-20 minutes or until cooked when tested with a skewer. Stand muffins in tin for 5 minutes before turning out onto a wire rack to cool. Serve dusted with icing sugar.
NOTE: You can store these muffins in an airtight container for up to 3 days. Alternatively, freeze for up to 1 month.

▶**TIP**
You will need 2 small carrots for this recipe.

Mini pea frittatas

 ProPoints VALUE PER FRITTATA | **MAKES:** 24 | **PREP:** 15 MINS | **COOKING TIME:** 15 MINS | SUITABLE TO FREEZE

▲ **6 eggs**
¼ cup (60ml) light thickened cream
▲ **¾ cup (90g) frozen peas, thawed**
▲ **2 green shallots, thinly sliced**
50g reduced-fat feta cheese, crumbled
▲ **¼ cup finely chopped fresh mint leaves**

Filling & Healthy Foods are marked with a green triangle.
These foods help fill you up and keep you healthy.

1 Preheat oven to 200°C or 180°C fan-forced.
Lightly spray two 12-hole (1 tablespoon/20ml
capacity) mini muffin tins with oil.
2 Whisk eggs and cream in a large jug. Season
with salt and freshly ground black pepper.
Add peas, shallots, feta and mint and stir to
combine. Pour mixture into prepared tin holes.
Bake for 15-20 minutes or until golden and cooked
through. Serve warm or cold.

NOTE: You can store these frittatas in an airtight
container in the fridge for up to 3 days.
Alternatively, freeze for up to 3 months.

Finger buns

 ProPoints VALUES PER BUN | **MAKES:** 16 | **PREP:** 20 MINS, PLUS 1 HOUR 20 MINS PROVING | **COOKING TIME:** 15 MINS, PLUS COOLING

2 cups (300g) plain flour
▲ 1 tsp ground cinnamon
⅓ cup (75g) caster sugar
2 tsp dried yeast
1 tsp canola oil
1 tsp vanilla extract
1 cup (160g) icing sugar
1 tbs Weight Watchers Canola Spread
2–3 drops red food colouring
1 tbs desiccated coconut

Filling & Healthy Foods are marked with a green triangle.
These foods help fill you up and keep you healthy.

1 Sift flour and cinnamon into a large mixing bowl. Stir in sugar and yeast. Combine oil, vanilla and ¾ cup (185ml) warm water in a jug (see tip). Add to flour mixture and mix until well combined. Knead dough on a lightly floured surface for 10 minutes or until smooth and elastic.
2 Lightly spray a large bowl with oil. Place dough in bowl and lightly spray top with oil. Cover with plastic wrap and place in a warm place for 1 hour or until dough has doubled in size.
3 Preheat oven to 180°C or 160°C fan-forced. Line 2 baking trays with baking paper. Punch down dough with your hand. Knead on a lightly floured surface for 1-2 minutes or until smooth and elastic. Divide dough into 16 equal portions and roll each portion into 10cm-long logs.
4 Place logs, 5cm apart, on prepared trays. Cover with a clean tea towel and place in a warm place for 20 minutes or until risen. Bake buns for 15-20 minutes or until golden and cooked through. Transfer to a wire rack to cool.
5 Place icing sugar and spread in a medium bowl. Gradually add 1 tablespoon warm water and stir until thick and smooth. Stir in enough food colouring for desired colour. Spread icing over buns and sprinkle with coconut. Serve.
NOTE: You can store these buns in an airtight container for up to 3 days.

▶ **TIP**
Use lukewarm water – if it's too hot it will kill the yeast and the dough will not rise.

Mexican dip with corn chips

 ProPoints VALUES PER SERVE | **SERVES:** 4 | **PREP:** 15 MINS | **COOKING TIME:** 5 MINS

2 slices corn mountain bread
½ medium avocado, mashed
▲ **1 tbs finely chopped fresh coriander leaves**
▲ **2 tsp finely chopped red onion**
▲ **1 tsp lime juice**
▲ **400g can red kidney beans, rinsed, drained**
▲ **2 tsp ground cumin**
▲ **½ cup (120g) fat-free natural yoghurt**
▲ **Pinch ground paprika**

Filling & Healthy Foods are marked with a green triangle.
These foods help fill you up and keep you healthy.

1 Preheat oven to 200°C or 180°C fan-forced. Place 1 slice of mountain bread on top of the other. Use kitchen scissors to cut bread stack into 3 long strips. Then cut each strip into 5 pieces to make 30 rectangles (about 6cm x 5cm). Place bread pieces on 2 large baking trays and lightly spray with oil. Bake for 2-3 minutes each side or until corn chips are golden and crisp.

2 Meanwhile, combine avocado, coriander, onion and juice in a small bowl. Season with salt and freshly ground pepper.

3 Place beans in a food processor with 2 tablespoons water and cumin. Process until smooth, adding a little more water to get a spreadable consistency. Spoon bean puree into the middle of a serving plate. Top with avocado mixture and yoghurt. Sprinkle with paprika. Serve dip with corn chips.

FEEL LIKE A FIESTA? THEN WHIP UP THIS
RUSTIC MEXICAN-STYLE DIP AND HOMEMADE
CORN CHIPS AND YOU CAN BE READY TO PARTY
IN 20 MINUTES OR LESS.

Zucchini, ham & chive pikelets

 ProPoints VALUES PER PIKELET | **MAKES:** 12 | **PREP:** 15 MINS | **COOKING TIME:** 10 MINS

½ cup (75g) self-raising flour
¼ cup (35g) wholemeal self-raising flour
▲ ½ cup (125ml) skim milk
▲ 1 egg, lightly beaten
▲ 1 tbs finely chopped fresh chives
▲ 1 small zucchini, grated
▲ 2 slices (42g) 97% fat-free ham, chopped
1 tbs olive oil

Filling & Healthy Foods are marked with a green triangle. These foods help fill you up and keep you healthy.

1 Combine flours in a medium bowl. Make a well in the centre. Whisk milk, egg and chives in a medium jug. Pour egg mixture into well in flour mixture and whisk until just smooth. Stir in zucchini and ham.

2 Heat half the oil in a large non-stick frying pan over medium-high heat. Drop 1 heaped tablespoon of batter into pan. Repeat to make 6 pikelets. Cook for 2 minutes or until bubbles rise to the surface. Turn and cook for 1 minute or until golden and cooked through. Repeat with remaining oil and batter to make 12 pikelets. Serve.

SERVE WITH: Chive yoghurt. Mix ½ cup (140g) no-fat Greek-style natural yoghurt with 1 tablespoon finely chopped fresh chives. Add 2 **ProPoints** values per serve for 1 tablespoon.

Easy sausage rolls

 ProPoints VALUES PER PIECE | **MAKES:** 21 | **PREP:** 15 MINS | **COOKING TIME:** 15 MINS | SUITABLE TO FREEZE

**2 sheets frozen reduced-fat puff pastry,
  just thawed**
7 (500g) reduced-fat pork sausages (see tip)
▲ **1 egg, lightly beaten**
1 tsp sesame seeds

Filling & Healthy Foods are marked with a green triangle.
These foods help fill you up and keep you healthy.

1 Preheat oven to 200°C or 180°C fan-forced. Line
a large baking tray with baking paper. Cut pastry
sheets into quarters. Discard 1 quarter to make
7 even-sized squares.
2 Place a sausage in the centre of each pastry
square. Brush edges of pastry with a little egg. Roll
pastry to enclose sausages. Trim any excess pastry
at the ends. Arrange rolls, seam-side-down, on
prepared tray. Brush with egg and sprinkle with
sesame seeds.
3 Bake for 12–15 minutes or until pastry is golden
brown and sausages are cooked through. Cool
slightly. Using a serrated knife, cut each sausage
roll into 3 pieces. Serve warm.
NOTE: Uncooked sausage rolls suitable to freeze
for up to 2 months.
SERVE WITH: Ready-made tomato chutney.
A 1 teaspoon serve is 0 **ProPoints** value.

▶ **TIP**
*You can use any flavour of
reduced-fat pork sausage for this
recipe. The **ProPoints** values
remain the same.*

Mini Thai chicken patties

 ProPoints VALUES PER PATTY | **MAKES:** 20 | **PREP:** 15 MINS | **COOKING TIME:** 15 MINS | SUITABLE TO FREEZE

500g lean chicken mince
▲ **2 green shallots, finely chopped**
▲ **¼ cup finely chopped fresh coriander leaves**
▲ **1 tsp finely grated lime rind**
▲ **2 tbs lime juice**
2 tbs sweet chilli sauce
3 tsp fish sauce
2 tsp brown sugar

Filling & Healthy Foods are marked with a green triangle.
These foods help fill you up and keep you healthy.

1 Place mince, shallots, coriander and rind in a large bowl. Season with salt and freshly ground black pepper and mix until combined. Roll rounded tablespoons of mixture into balls and flatten slightly to form 20 small patties.
2 Combine juice, sweet chilli and fish sauces and brown sugar in a small bowl. Stir until sugar has dissolved. Set dipping sauce aside.
3 Lightly spray a large non-stick frying pan with oil and heat over medium heat. Cook patties, in batches, for 3 minutes each side or until cooked through. Serve with dipping sauce.
NOTE: Uncooked patties suitable to freeze for up to 1 month.

▶ **TIP**
*You can use lean pork mince instead of chicken mince. The **ProPoints** values remain the same.*

Baby chocolate butterfly cakes

 ProPoints VALUES PER CAKE | **MAKES:** 24 | **PREP:** 30 MINS | **COOKING TIME:** 15 MINS, PLUS COOLING
SUITABLE TO FREEZE

1 cup (150g) self-raising flour
4 tbs cocoa powder
¼ cup (35g) caster sugar
½ cup (125ml) buttermilk
▲ 1 egg
60g Weight Watchers Canola Spread, melted
100g extra-light cream cheese
2 tbs icing sugar, plus extra to dust

Filling & Healthy Foods are marked with a green triangle.
These foods help fill you up and keep you healthy.

1 Preheat oven to 180°C or 160°C fan-forced. Line
two 12-hole (1½ tablespoon/30ml capacity) mini
muffin tins with paper cases.
2 Sift flour and half the cocoa into a large mixing
bowl. Stir in caster sugar. Whisk buttermilk, egg
and spread in a medium bowl until combined.
Add to flour mixture and stir until just combined
(do not over-mix).
3 Spoon mixture into prepared cases. Bake for
15-20 minutes or until cooked when tested with a
skewer. Stand cakes in tins for 5 minutes before
turning out onto a wire rack to cool.
4 Using electric beaters, beat cream cheese in
a medium bowl until smooth. Gradually add
2 tablespoons icing sugar and remaining cocoa
and beat until smooth. Cut tops from cooled cakes
and set aside. Top cakes with cream cheese
mixture. Cut cake tops in half and position in
cream cheese mixture to create butterfly wings.
Serve dusted with icing sugar.
NOTE: Unfilled cakes suitable to freeze for up to
1 month.

Cranberry & orange biscotti

 ProPoints VALUES PER BISCOTTI | **MAKES:** 20 | **PREP:** 15 MINS | **COOKING TIME:** 35 MINS, PLUS COOLING

⅓ cup (75g) caster sugar
▲ 1 egg
1 cup (150g) plain flour
▲ 1 tsp finely grated orange rind
⅓ cup (40g) finely chopped macadamia nuts
⅓ cup (45g) dried cranberries

Filling & Healthy Foods are marked with a green triangle.
These foods help fill you up and keep you healthy.

1 Preheat oven to 180°C or 160°C fan-forced. Line a large baking tray with baking paper.
2 Using electric beaters, beat sugar and egg in a small bowl for 2–3 minutes or until thick and creamy. Gently fold in flour until just combined. Fold in rind, macadamias and cranberries.
3 Place mixture on a lightly floured surface and shape into a 20cm-long log. Place log on prepared tray and flatten slightly until 4cm thick. Bake for 20 minutes or until firm. Cool.
4 Reduce oven to 140°C or 120°C fan-forced. Using a serrated knife, cut log into 1cm-thick slices. Place slices, in a single layer, on tray and bake, turning halfway through cooking, for 15–20 minutes or until crisp and golden. Transfer biscotti to wire racks to cool. Serve.

▶ **TIP**
You can store this biscotti in an airtight container for up to 2 weeks.

Cinnamon teacake

 ProPoints VALUES PER SERVE | **SERVES:** 8 | **PREP:** 15 MINS | **COOKING TIME:** 25 MINS

90g Weight Watchers Canola Spread
½ cup (110g) caster sugar, plus 2 tsp
    for topping
▲ 1 egg
2 tsp vanilla bean paste (see note)
1 cup (150g) self-raising flour, sifted
▲ ⅓ cup (80ml) skim milk
▲ ½ tsp ground cinnamon

Filling & Healthy Foods are marked with a green triangle.
These foods help fill you up and keep you healthy.

1 Preheat oven to 180°C or 160°C fan-forced. Lightly spray a 20cm round cake tin with oil. Line base and side with baking paper.

2 Using electric beaters, beat 75g spread, ½ cup (110g) sugar, egg and vanilla bean paste in a medium bowl until combined. Mix in flour and milk, alternately, until combined.

3 Spread mixture into prepared tin and smooth the surface. Bake for 25-30 minutes or until cooked when tested with a skewer. Stand cake in tin for 5 minutes before turning out, top-side up, onto a wire rack.

4 Place remaining spread in a small microwave-safe bowl and microwave on Medium (50%) for 30 seconds or until melted. Combine cinnamon and 2 teaspoons sugar in a small bowl. Brush hot cake with melted spread. Sprinkle with cinnamon sugar. Serve warm or cold.

NOTE: Vanilla bean paste is sold in jars in the baking aisle of most supermarkets.

▶ **TIP**
This cake is best served on the day it is made.

AS YOU SPRINKLE THE SUGARY TOPPING
ONTO THE STILL-HOT CAKE THE
SEDUCTIVELY SWEET SCENT OF
CINNAMON WILL FILL THE AIR.

10 Simple treat ideas

1 Coriander & lemon hommus with asparagus dippers

 ProPoints VALUES PER SERVE | **SERVES:** 1

Cook ▲ **½ bunch asparagus** in a saucepan of boiling water for 1 minute or until just tender. Refresh in cold water. Drain. Combine ▲ **1 tbs chopped fresh coriander leaves**, ▲ **1 tsp lemon rind**, ▲ **1 tsp lemon juice** and **¼ cup reduced-fat hommus** in a small bowl. Serve with asparagus.

---

2 Choc cranberry trail mix

 ProPoints VALUES PER SERVE | **SERVES:** 1

Combine **1 square fine 70% cocoa dark chocolate** (chopped), **6 raw almonds** (chopped), **20g dried cranberries** and **3 tsp pepitas** (pumpkin seed kernels) in a small bowl. Serve.

---

3 Dukkah egg on crispbread

 ProPoints VALUES PER SERVE | **SERVES:** 1

Spread ▲ **2 wholegrain crispbreads** with **1 tsp Weight Watchers Canola Spread**. Top with ▲ **1 hard boiled egg** (sliced) and sprinkle with **1 tsp dukkah** and ▲ **¼ cup alfalfa sprouts**. Serve.
NOTE: Dukkah is a mix of nuts, seeds and spices used in Middle Eastern cooking. Find it in the spice aisle of most supermarkets.

4 Ricotta honey apricots

 ProPoints VALUES PER SERVE | **SERVES:** 1

Halve ▲ **2 fresh apricots** and remove stones. Combine ▲ **2 tbs low-fat smooth ricotta cheese**, **1 tsp honey**, **⅛ tsp vanilla extract** and a ▲ **pinch cinnamon** in a small bowl. Fill apricot halves with ricotta mixture. Serve.

---

5 Tuna lettuce cups

 ProPoints VALUES PER SERVE | **SERVES:** 1

Combine ▲ **95g can tuna in springwater** (drained, flaked), ▲ **2 tsp lemon juice**, ▲ **½ carrot** (grated), ▲ **1 tbs chopped fresh chives**, **1 tsp baby capers** (rinsed, drained) and **1 gherkin** (finely chopped) in a small bowl. Spoon into ▲ **2 lettuce cups** to serve.

---

6 Moroccan pita chips & mint yoghurt

 ProPoints VALUES PER SERVE | **SERVES:** 1

Preheat oven to 180°C or 160°C fan-forced. Combine ▲ **¼ cup low-fat natural yoghurt**, ▲ **½ tsp ground cumin** and ▲ **1 tbs chopped fresh mint leaves** in a small bowl. Lightly spray **1 x 68g wholemeal pita bread** with oil and sprinkle with **2 tsp Moroccan seasoning**. Bake bread for 5-6 minutes or until crisp. Break into pieces and serve with mint yoghurt.

7 Chilli cheese popcorn

 ProPoints VALUES PER SERVE | **SERVES:** 1

Combine ▲ **1 cup air-popped popcorn**, **1 tbs finely grated parmesan cheese** and ▲ **¼ tsp dried red chilli flakes** in a small bowl. Serve.

---

8 Apple, cinnamon & cottage cheese muffin

 ProPoints VALUES PER SERVE | **SERVES:** 1

Spread **1 wholemeal English muffin** (split, toasted) with ▲ **2 tbs low-fat cottage cheese**. Top with ▲ **1 red apple** (grated) and sprinkle with ▲ **ground cinnamon**. Serve.

---

9 Blueberry walnut yoghurt swirl

 ProPoints VALUES PER SERVE | **SERVES:** 1

Scoop ▲ **150g tub Nestlé Soleil Vanilla Flavoured Yoghurt** into a bowl. Add ▲ **1 cup fresh blueberries** (lightly crushed) and **1 tbs chopped walnuts** and swirl through yoghurt. Serve.

10 Tahini pecan pumpkin

 ProPoints VALUES PER SERVE | **SERVES:** 1

Steam or microwave ▲ **1 cup chopped pumpkin** until tender. Combine ▲ **¼ cup low-fat natural yoghurt**, **2 tsp tahini paste** and ▲ **1 tbs lemon juice** in a small bowl. Drizzle tahini yoghurt over pumpkin and sprinkle with **3 pecans** (chopped). Serve.
NOTE: Tahini paste is made from crushed sesame seeds. Find it in the health-food aisle of most supermarkets.

Grab 'n' go snacks

unger has a habit of creeping up on you – those tummy rumbles can occur at any time, any place. Trying to ignore them often doesn't work, so it's better to nibble on a low **ProPoints** value snack that will keep your weight loss on track. The key is to make sure you have lots of healthy snacks available in your kitchen and take them with you whenever you head out the door. Here is a list of some of our favourite snack options to enjoy at home or on the go.

ProPoints 0 VALUE PER SERVING

- ½ x 250g punnet strawberries.
- 10 cherry tomatoes.
- 2 fresh dates.
- Diet lime cordial with soda water.
- Peppermint herbal tea.
- 1 cup cherries.
- 1 cup steamed vegetables (excludes potatoes, parsnip, corn, green peas).
- 1 cup grapes.
- 1 tub fresh fruit salad.
- 1 custard apple.
- 1 serve (125ml) Weight Watchers Jelly (any flavour).
- Vegie sticks – carrot, cucumber, celery, capsicum, asparagus.
- 1 cup blueberries.
- 0 **ProPoints** value garden salad.
- 1 serve (133g) Weight Watchers Halved Apricots, drained.
- 135g tub Weight Watchers Apricot Fruit Snack.

ProPoints 1 VALUE PER SERVING

- 1 slice (21g) Bega So Extra Light tasty cheese.
- 1 cup (15g) air-popped popcorn.
- ½ cup (60g) frozen peas, boiled.
- 1 cup (250ml) miso soup.
- 135g tub Weight Watchers Peaches with Mango Puree Fruit Snack.
- 1 teaspoon sunflower seeds.
- 20g packet Continental Cup A Soup Classic Chicken Noodle made following packet instructions.
- 2 dried pitted dates.
- 1 water iceblock (any flavour).
- 6 kalamata olives in brine, drained.
- 2 teaspoons pepitas (pumpkin seed kernels).
- 2 (12g) wholegrain crispbreads.
- 10 unsalted pistachio nut kernels.
- ½ x 32g packet Weight Watchers Fruities (any flavour).
- 6 dried apricot halves.
- ¼ cup (45g) cooked chickpeas.

ProPoints 2
VALUE PER SERVING

- 1 medium boiled egg.
- 10 (17g) seaweed rice crackers.
- 2 (25g) brown rice cakes.
- 1 pkt Weight Watchers Drinking Chocolate made following packet instructions with 200ml hot water.
- 25g Weight Watchers Choc Crisp Original bar.
- 20g pkt Country Cup Creamy Potato & Leek Soup made following packet instructions.
- 1 slice (35g) wholemeal fruit loaf.
- 1 serve (175ml) Weight Watchers Berry Flavoured Mousse.
- 1 serve (125ml) Weight Watchers Dessert Mix (any flavour).
- 40g Weis Mango & Ice Cream mini bar.
- 1 slice (35g) mixed grain bread.
- 20g packet Carman's Muesli Bites (any flavour).
- 19g packet Weight Watchers Nibblies (any flavour).
- 20g packet Weight Watchers Potato Bakes Sour Cream and Chives Flavour.
- 1 small (250ml) skim-milk cappuccino or latte.
- 5 pieces dried apple.
- 105g Streets Calippo iceblock (any flavour).
- 62g tub Nestlé Soleil Chocolate Mousse.
- 28g Weight Watchers Rich Toffee Bar.
- 23g Weight Watchers Carrot Cake Slice.
- 22g packet Uncle Tobys Le Snak.

ProPoints 3
VALUE PER SERVING

- 16 raw almonds.
- 130g can Weight Watchers Baked Beans.
- 10 banana chips.
- 15 (25g) rice crackers (any flavour).
- 3 dried apricots and 2 Brazil nuts.
- 37.5g Weight Watchers Fruit Cereal Bar (any flavour).
- 200g low-fat natural yoghurt.
- 1 (120g) corn on the cob (no butter).
- 31g Uncle Tobys Apricot Chewy Muesli Bar.
- 25g bhuja mix (Indian savoury nibble mix).
- 40g dried cranberries.
- 145ml tub Weight Watchers Ice Cream (any flavour).
- 1 (30g) Mini Babybel Cheese.

ProPoints 4
VALUE PER SERVING

- 1 handful (30g) mixed fruit and nuts.
- 5 Brazil nuts.
- 1 mini (50g) apple and oatbran reduced-fat muffin.
- 1 (100g) tuna or smoked salmon sushi roll.
- 25g unsalted roasted peanuts.
- 40g Uncle Tobys Weightwise Oats, prepared with ¾ cup (185ml) skim milk.

Index *The Complete Kitchen*

* Mini meal idea recipe

	PAGE	ProPoints
Ginger chocolate mousse*	135	4
Grilled maple peach with hazelnuts*	134	3
Melon salad with passionfruit yoghurt*	134	1
Passionfruit & coconut crème brûlées	123	5
Pavlova with berries & raspberry sauce	120	5
Pineapple, macadamia & coconut yoghurt parfait*	134	4
Spiced poached pears with nutmeg custard*	135	3
Summer pudding	126	7
Watermelon, strawberries & rosewater ice-cream*	135	4

DRESSINGS, MARINADES & SPICE RUBS

	PAGE	ProPoints
Barbecue spice rub	27	1
French dressing	26	1
Greek marinade	27	1
Honey soy marinade	27	2
Italian dressing	26	1
Lemon & chilli marinade	27	1
Moroccan spice rub	27	0
Sweet chilli & lime dressing	26	1

EGGS

	PAGE	ProPoints
Bacon & egg muffin*	46	6
B.E.S.T. breakfast burger	39	9
Dukkah egg on crispbread*	152	5
Egg, avocado & dukkah on rye*	46	7
French toast 2 ways (sweet/savoury)	44	9/8
Mini pea frittatas	140	1
Mushroom quiche	105	4
Pavlova with berries & raspberry sauce	120	5
Persian eggs with feta & sumac	42	7
Poached green eggs & ham	35	7
Satay egg & chicken salad wrap	62	8
Spinach & ricotta omelette*	46	7
Tuna & egg pasta salad*	73	9
Tuna & spinach tarts	53	5

FISH & SEAFOOD

	PAGE	ProPoints
Baked salmon with cherry tomatoes, olives & capers	92	11
Coriander salmon with sweet chilli sauce*	116	12
Couscous salad with tuna, tomatoes, olives & rocket	63	9
Easy pork & prawn larb	110	8
Fish tacos with cabbage & coriander slaw	85	9
Fragrant baked fish	99	4
Italian platter*	73	10
Mackerel & coriander brown rice salad*	72	9
Poached salmon with asparagus & puy lentils	55	9
Prawn, cucumber & watercress baguette	54	11
Salmon & cream cheese crispbreads*	72	7
Spaghetti marinara	94	14
Toasted rye with spicy avocado, salmon & snow pea shoots	60	7
Tuna & egg pasta salad*	73	9
Tuna & spinach tarts	53	5
Tuna lettuce cups*	152	3
Tuna mornay	88	12
Yellow snapper with coriander rice & vegies*	117	7

FRUIT

	PAGE	ProPoints
Apple, cinnamon & cottage cheese muffin*	153	4
Apricot crumble tarts	124	4
Baked apple with dates & walnuts*	135	4
Baked apples with pecans & fig	129	4
Banana & walnut cereal biscuits*	47	7
Banana ice-cream*	134	0
Berries with honey & spice ricotta*	134	3
Blueberry banana creams	133	1
Blueberry walnut yoghurt swirl*	153	2
Carrot & banana muffins	138	4
Cheat's Danish with poached apricots	37	7
Cherry choc meringue*	134	5
Cherry yoghurt iceblocks	132	1
Choc cranberry trail mix*	152	5
Choc-orange baklava stacks	131	5
French toast 2 ways – sweet	44	9
Grilled maple peach with hazelnuts*	134	3
Melon salad with passionfruit yoghurt*	134	1
Pan-fried pork with pears*	116	8
Passionfruit & coconut crème brûlées	123	5
Pavlova with berries & raspberry sauce	120	5
Pear, pecan & coconut porridge*	47	8
Pineapple, macadamia & coconut yoghurt parfait*	134	4
Plum & almond crumpets*	46	7
Quinoa bircher muesli	43	7
Raspberry hotcakes	40	7
Ricotta honey apricots*	152	2

Index The Complete Kitchen

* Mini meal idea recipe

kitchen notes

Not sure what equipment you need or how to freeze your leftovers? You'll find everything you need to cook Weight Watchers recipes right here.

To create these delicious recipes you'll need:

- A can of oil spray (available in the oil aisle of supermarkets).
- A non-stick frying pan (used in more than 50 per cent of these recipes).
- An Australian metric jug for measuring liquids (250ml = 1 cup).
- A set of four Australian metric measuring cups (1 cup = 250ml, ½ cup = 125ml, ⅓ cup = 80ml and ¼ cup = 60ml) for measuring dry ingredients such as flour, sugar, rice etc.
- A set of four Australian metric measuring spoons (1 tablespoon = 20ml, 1 teaspoon = 5ml, ½ teaspoon and ¼ teaspoon) for small liquid and dry ingredients.
- Metric scales for weighing correct portions of meat, chicken, fish and seafood and other foods that don't fit in a cup.

More quick tips:

- Read the recipe all the way through and get out everything you need before you start cooking.
- For accurate results, ensure cup and spoon measurements are level (use the back of a knife to level off dry ingredients).
- We use eggs with an average weight of 59g in these recipes (usually sold as 'extra large').

Freezer guide

Freezing food is a great way to store leftovers or ensure you always have a healthy meal on standby for busy days. We've marked which recipes in this book are suitable to freeze - here's a basic how-to guide:

FOOD TYPE	HOW TO STORE	HOW LONG?
Liquid-based meals (stews, soups, curries, ratatouille, ragu). Omit any cream or yoghurt and add when reheating.	Cool and place in freezerproof containers, leaving 2–3cm at the top for expansion. Label with name, date and number of serves.	3 months
Whole dishes (lasagne, cottage pie, pasta bakes).	Cook in a freezerproof, ovenproof dish. Cool, then wrap entire dish in a double layer of plastic wrap. Wrap in foil. Label with name, date and number of serves.	2 months
Baked goods (unfilled cakes, muffins, slices, fruit and banana breads, pikelets, pancakes).	Cool, then double wrap in plastic wrap (either in individual serves or whole). Wrap in foil. Label with name, date and number of serves.	1 month
Raw patties & cooked fritters	Cool, then separate with squares of baking paper. Double wrap in plastic wrap. Wrap in foil. Label with name, date and number of serves.	1 month
Poached fruit	Cool and place in freezerproof containers, leaving 2–3cm at the top for expansion. Label with name, date and number of serves.	6 months

Food with a low moisture content (cakes and muffins) can be thawed at room temperature. Food with a high moisture content (liquid-based meals and raw meat, chicken and seafood) must be thawed overnight in the fridge.

SENIOR FOOD EDITOR: *Lucy Kelly*
ASSISTANT FOOD EDITOR: *Cathie Lonnie*
PHOTOGRAPHY: *Vanessa Levis, Steve Brown*
STYLING: *Marie-Hélène Clauzon*
FOOD PREPARATION: *Kerrie Ray*
RECIPE DEVELOPMENT: *Peta Dent, Chrissy Freer, Cathie Lonnie, Gemma Luongo, Liz Macri, Sally Parker, Kirrily La Rosa, Tracy Rutherford*
FOOD COMPLIANCE MANAGER: *Kristine Iligan*
NUTRITION COMMUNICATIONS MANAGERS: *Roslyn Anderson, Ana Riberio*
FOOD CONTENT ADMINISTRATOR: *Nour Nazha*
ADVERTISING & PUBLISHING COORDINATOR: *Yara Oulabi*
NATIONAL CORPORATE ADVERTISING MANAGER: *Marion Sheehan*
SENIOR BUSINESS MANAGER PUBLISHING: *Faye James*
COMMERCIAL DIRECTOR: *Tony Karras*

WEIGHT WATCHERS AUSTRALIA:
LOCKED BAG 2020,
BROADWAY NSW 2007
PHONE: 13 19 97
WEIGHTWATCHERS.COM.AU

WEIGHT WATCHERS NZ:
PO BOX 1328, AUCKLAND
PHONE: 0900 009 131
WEIGHTWATCHERS.CO.NZ

PUBLISHED BY ACP MAGAZINES LIMITED, UNDER ARRANGEMENT WITH WEIGHT WATCHERS INTERNATIONAL, INC.
PRODUCED BY ACP CUSTOM MEDIA, A DIVISION OF ACP MAGAZINES LTD
LEVEL 18, 66-68 GOULBURN STREET, SYDNEY 2000
PHONE: (02) 9282 8000
FAX: (02) 9267 3625
EDITOR: *Tracey Platt*
ART DIRECTOR: *Sally Keane*
PRODUCTION COORDINATOR: *Rachel Walsh*
PREPRESS TEAM LEADER: *Peter Suchecki*

ACP CORPORATE
CHIEF EXECUTIVE OFFICER ACP MAGAZINES: *Matthew Stanton*
PUBLISHING DIRECTOR ACP MAGAZINES: *Gerry Reynolds*

ACP CUSTOM MEDIA
PUBLISHER ACP CUSTOM MEDIA & BOOKS: *Sally Wright*
PUBLISHING MANAGER: *Nicola O'Hanlon*

NINE ENTERTAINMENT CO.
CHIEF EXECUTIVE OFFICER: *David Gyngell*
GROUP SALES AND MARKETING DIRECTOR: *Peter Wiltshire*

PRINTED BY TOPPAN PRINTING CO, CHINA.

I'm feeling it

With a thick, delicious taste and all the confidence of no fat and
low sugar,* you'll be feeling it with Nestlé® Soleil.™

Mealtimes made easy

Whether you're looking for low-fat alternatives to everyday ingredients, portion controlled snacks, ready-to-eat meals or decadent desserts, the Weight Watchers® foods range has you covered.

Our fantastic supermarket product range offers an amazing variety of options and flavours for every meal – from breakfast to dinner (and those times in between)! Every pack features the exact **ProPoints®** values making food tracking quick and easy. You'll love the convenience and great taste of these weight-loss friendly products. For more details, visit weightwatchersfoods.com.au / co.nz